IS THE PRIZE WORHT THE PRICE?

DALE RULE

DEDICATION

To my best friend and dedicated wife, Lya: Without your love, prayers, and patience this book would not have been possible.

Also to my boys, Joey, Jeffery, and Josh: May you all become incredible men of influence and impact! May your lives be filled with an abundance of love and happiness just as you bring to your mom and I.

INTRODUCTION

My survival became my story, My story ignited my passion, My passion drives my vision, My vision is blessed by God's Grace!

Is the Prize worth the Price? The journey of a life that has been changed forever just by going for a walk. As I start this story it is November 2013 and I am 41. I will have a few key dates and fill in around them in my ongoing journey of saving my own life.

Just a heads up I am writing this book while working out or after a workout. I pray when working out, asking God to guide my words and thoughts. I am writing each day from where my heart is at that moment, so there a few off subject thoughts, rants and an occasional A.D.D.

moment in the middle of my story or time in my life. I will talk about God and Jesus throughout because my faith is major part of my story. My hope is you don't miss the message because of the delivery. I am not here to preach only to share. Thank you for taking the time to read I hope you don't get too lost in some of the randomness. God Bless Dale

Chapter 1

"Is the Prize worth the Price?" Dale Rule

Following is a timeline of my weight loss journey from 363 lbs to 219 lbs in 14 months. On December 18, 2009 I weighed 363 pounds. On February 10 2010 I weighed 335 pounds (the first day I went for a walk!). On August 10 2010 I weighed 233 pounds (goal was 100 pounds in 6 months). Dec of 2010 I weighed in at 223 pounds (140 pounds in 1 year). February 10 2011 I weighed 219 pounds. Two and a half years later the weight is still off and the fight (price and prize) continues.

This journey is accomplished 1 step at a time. Walking daily and continuing to be aware of how much I am eating, an incredible support structure, and a driven passion to save my own life. What follows are true life events.

Is the PRIZE worth the PRICE? I have been coaching high school football for 24 years and this is something I have said to many players many times when it came to the commitment it took to reach the goals that they had set for themselves. Set a goal or aspiration (prize) for the person/player you want to be, then in detail write down and understand what it looks like to reach the goal (price).

What does each day of the off season look like? What is your lifting program, fitness program, skill improvement program, rest and recovery, having fun, family time, being a kid? Success at anything (prize) is a direct relationship to the work and commitment (price) you personally are willing to put in. I share this because the thing I had been talking to kids about for 20 years I had not been living, and at 37 years old and 363 pounds I was literally killing myself. After lying to myself for so long that I was unselfish I finally realized I was the most selfish person I knew in all the wrong areas. I am very blessed with an incredible wife Lya (17 years in 2013 and counting) and 3 amazing sons Joey, Jeffery, and Josh. What I realized is that my selfishness was going to leave them without me in their lives. The path I was headed down I would be lucky to see my grandchildren born. I honestly believe if God had not planted that seed to go for a walk on February 10th I would be over 400 pounds today.

Chapter 2

"You tell yourself something long enough you start to believe it!" Chad Veach

I often get asked what was the trigger that caused you to change? What health crises caused the change? As I look back and have answered many, many times there really was not one. The closest thing would be a picture that was taken in San Francisco at a Monday night football game with my wife. I saw the picture right after it was taken and thought to myself, wow I am really big. (Pants 56 inch waste, 3x sweatshirt) We were in San Francisco because I had meetings for work there. I was a district manager for Jack in the Box. I remember driving home to Camas, Washington and every once in a while I would think about that picture. The morning after we got home I got on the scale and weighed 363 pounds the biggest that I had ever seen on a scale for me. It had a small impact. I would be a little more aware of what I was eating, but I love food, worked in the food industry, and it was the holidays. You know all the good excuses (selfishness, wrong prize) I had always used. I still managed to lose about 14 pounds in December. Besides January was coming and I would just start another News Years resolution but this time it would work right!?

January 2010 comes around and here I go, I am going to eat better and exercise. Here is a key sign that it would not work this time either. I had been over 300 pounds for 10 years and every single January I lost weight and by March I had gained it back plus some. I never had structure I would just wing it. I knew the Prize but never committed go the Price. On a side note I knew I had it in me to change. January 2009 is the last day I have had a single drink of soda. (Quit cold turkey) I was addicted to Dr. Pepper, I woke up every morning and ended everyday with one. The fact that it was free at my job made it easier. I drank anywhere from 4000 to 7000 calories a day just in soda. (1 16oz bottle of Dr. Pepper is 250 calories) So a minimum of 15 bottles a day. I would drink a 32 oz cup approximately each hour (500 empty calories) I was at work. More on calories consumed in a day to come just got side tracked. So back to January I was committed just like every other year. No more fried food, no more chips, no more junk food, more salad and veggies. Well that lasted about a month with some slips here and there. The reality for me was by early February my habits around food were becoming the norm for me again. Then a very important conversation happened at the Sea Tac airport with a colleague of mine Garry Siggelkow.

Garry also worked for Jack in the Box and we were all

in Seattle for a meeting early February 2010. Garry worked in Boise Idaho so I would see Garry 4 to 5 times a year at meetings, as well as spend a couple weeks each year in San Diego together. Garry and I both served on a leadership council for our regions. Garry was never what I would consider obese like I was but Garry had battled weight off and on. I noticed that about 2 years earlier from 1 meeting to the next, Garry had really lost some weight and got lean. I had talked with Garry 3 or 4 times before our meeting at the airport about how he lost the weight and how he was keeping it off. Garry would tell me about his workout routine and how he was eating. All of what he told me, I had tried to some degree in the previous years.

I remember sitting at a Denny's in Tigard, Oregon with Garry having breakfast he ordered oatmeal and fruit I had a ham and cheese omelet, hash browns, toast, and 3 pancakes with a soda! All while we were discussing how he lost weight and kept it off. I saw it was working for him but it was too strict for me (price to big) besides I worked full time, coached football, and had a family where would I find time. I did not realize at the time my Prize was wrong and not big enough and the Price I thought was too big!

Here is the difference this time when we were at the airport. Garry did not give me the details of what he did or did not do. Garry told me the structure he used. Garry had bought a BodyBugg through body media and 24 hour fitness. So that opened up a new dialog for Garry and me. I asked Garry every question I could about this thing I had no clue what it was I had seen the arm band being used on the show "Biggest Loser" but did not know what they were. I give Garry a lot of credit in understanding and caring about people. I had spoke with Garry on many occasions about weight loss and Garry never saw any changes in me so he changed the message and I finally heard him. Thank you Garry for being so selfless you had a major impact in saving my life.

Quick side note we were flying home from Seattle to Portland that day on Horizon air. It was a smaller plane and I was a big dude you know the kind you hope never sits by you on the plane. The one who out of embarrassment tries everything they can to buckle seat belt without an extender. Which by the way rarely works unless you get it just right under your belly and hope you never have to get up again on the flight! Anyway the plane had 2 seats on each side and it was assigned seating of which I had an aisle seat. The plane is about 95% loaded and there is no one next to me so I was thinking every big boys dream both seats are mine. Wouldn't you know it one of the last people on the plane had the seat next to me and this gentlemen was one of the nicest people you could ask to sit next to. He lived on the Oregon coast and flew helicopters for a living. He worked in the forest fire industry and would travel the U.S. and dump water buckets on fires from the helicopter. This gentleman was a former military pilot so he shared a lot of knowledge with me about the plane and the safety of a prop engine. It was a great conversation during the flight while we shared some tight space together. I share this because at the time I was 5'11" and around 335 pounds. The gentleman next to me was around 6'3" and over 300 pounds as well. Talk about a tight squeeze, we got to know each other well. The flight attendants were very helpful to us both even asking numerous people if they would switch seats which no one would so we made it work. Both needed seat belt extenders by the way. I had two close friends and colleagues on that flight they got a big kick out of that flight, thanks Jeff and Peter!

That evening when I get home I was very excited to look on line and learn more about this BodyBugg thing. My wife being the amazing person she is, listens to my rambling's about how this will finally be the thing that works, you know after trying everything else other than being committed and making life long changes. So we sit down and look at web site, Lya explains some of the technical things, and we order 2 one for each of us. On February 9, 2010 they arrived at the house and Lya set both of them up. When I got home that evening I begin setting up the plan with the BodyBugg. There are many things you can do, but for me personally the simpler the better. I already understood that if you burn 3500 calories more than you eat you would lose a pound. For example if you take in 2500 calories a day and burn 3000 calories a day you would lose a pound a week. Your daily calorie burn would be 500 more than you ate. Seven days times

500 calories equals a 3500 calorie deficit for the week equal to one pound lost. Right, simple math, but the key for me was how do I know what I burn a day? This is where the system gave me the structure I needed. I wore the arm band and downloaded it every night on my computer to get my estimated calorie burn based on my activity. This was a victory for me. I am very competitive so now I was competing against myself. On February 10, 2010 I set the goal to lose 100 pounds in 6 months.

Chapter 3

"Energy flows were your attention goes!" Pastor Dave McCabe

Throughout the 6 months the Price changed many times as I learned more about myself, food, and my commitment. The key is the Prize never changed! It was and still is to this day about a healthy life. I will say though through it all, the Prize got bigger and bigger but the foundation of the Prize is a healthy life.

Back to the beginning of my journey February 10, that evening after I got home from work my wife and I went out on a walk. Originally I told my wife I was going to walk for 2 hours. Walk 1 hour away from our house and follow the same path home for 2 hours total of walking. To be completely honest 5 minutes in I was done! We ended up walking 1 mile. My legs were cramping, my back hurt it all sucked! That was where I was. The path we ended up completing that first day was a half mile of a slight incline to my son's grade school then a half mile downhill home. We probably stopped 5 times on the way up. I was not in a good place complaining, cursing, embarrassed, ashamed, and angry. I even kicked a tree at one point I was so frustrated. Not very smart when walking, just added to the pain and now my foot hurt! About 15 minutes after starting to walk I told my wife that was far enough and I was ready to head home frustrated and defeated. I would have probably gone and ate to console myself. Then the most important moment happened, Lya yelled at me.

We had been married 13 years at the time so we had had our arguments and disagreements, but this was different. Rarely does Lya curse especially at me or at any person. She kind of laid into me only one curse word but I knew she meant business! I was not mad at Lya, I was encouraged by what she said. Lya has always supported everything I did especially around losing weight, and you name it I tried it, every weight loss plan, miracle drug, and quick fix. I always wanted the easy way not a behavior change. One example, before I even hit the big 300 pound mark in life. I was around 280 and started taking Metabalife and doing the Adkins diet at the same time. The results on the scale were incredible almost 60 pounds in 60 days! Every day I thought my heart was going to explode! It was scary but at the time it did not matter it was working and I still got to eat a lot of food. Within 8 months of losing the 60 pounds and stopping the pills I hit 300 pounds for the first time.

Back to the walk, Lya and I came to the agreement that I could make it to the School and back, if you can call it that she truly did not give me a choice! Thank you Lya, you changed my life that one moment of brutal honesty. We started back on the walk, and we made it to the school. Across the street there is a bench were I rested for 5 minutes contemplating life and the ability to breathe normal again. Now we headed back home which was still tough but easier being at a slight decline. That 1 mile adventure took 41 minutes to complete with at least 30 minutes of actual walking time. Once we got home I immediately went to the computer to download my BodyBugg and see what my calories burned were for the day. Victory! Not only did I meet my goal for the day I exceeded it. Remember I am very competitive so now I had a goal to shoot for every day.

When I programmed the BodyBugg system and set the goal to lose 100 pound in 6 months the program calculated the amount of calories I would have to burn above what I consumed each day. I set the goal to eat 1950

calories daily. I had no clue what 1950 calories looked like, but the BodyBugg has plans you can follow and guideline resources. I would use the resources to help me plan my food. I have never been a big fruits and veggies guy so I had a tough learning curve around food. The best part for me is I entered my food every day into the system. This really helped me learn about my behaviors, nothing like facing the truth by having it stare you in the face 5 or 6 times a day. Talk about the Price changing. One of the big things for me was I did not change all of what I ate. For the most part I changed the amount I ate. I will say though I only had a cheeseburger and fries one time in six months. I was committed to that calorie count and not exceeding 1950 in a day. There were a few days in that first month that I only ate two meals for the day as I learned, not ideal but I was focused. I found the ability to meet and exceed my daily calorie burn become very easy the more I kept at

it. I became addicted to walking.

The most important thing I did after the first walk on February 10, was go for a walk again on February 11. I walked that same mile route for 4 days then on the 5 day I walked it once in the morning and once in the evening. That became the minimum I would walk every day.

We lived in an area in Camas Washington known as Prune Hill so there were a lot challenging uphill walks I could take. We lived about 3/4 of the way up so if I walked to the bottom I would have to walk back up. I began to drive the area plotting out routes that round tripped back to my house. All had some challenging hills in them. I was addicted!

I need to share one obstacle or excuse I could have used and still have to overcome daily. I have had issues with cramping especially in my legs and back, since I was a young athlete. I worked out a lot but had poor nutrition

habits, and I always attributed my cramping to that. But as I got older the cramping got worse and affected my whole body. On 3 different occasions I started the process of getting answers. The first 2 times I got frustrated at the lack of answers after many tests and stop going to the doctor. I finally promised my wife I would follow through to the end and get the answers to what was going on. After two and a half years of testing, two muscle biopsies and countless doctor visits, my specialist told me that I was a medical anomaly. They had no answers other than I have a neurological disorder that affects my muscles, and that they would review my case yearly to see if anyone else has similar symptoms. So everyday can be an adventure and I have almost perfected the ability to get cramps out of any part of my body.

The worst cramping of all has happened on three different occasions over last two years. My inner thigh has

cramped so severely that it partially cut off blood flow from my femoral artery, causing me to partially pass out. The First time I was alone at my apartment in Denver. I was in Denver for work with Jack in the box. I started to cramp in my calf and inner thigh while I was sleeping. It is a regular occurrence for me to cramp up while sleeping, and I usually just jump out of bed and get the cramp out. This time was no different at first. I got out of bed real fast to get the muscles stretched out before they were fully cramped. After about 30 seconds I knew something was wrong. I was very light headed and then everything went a little crazy. For some reason all I wanted to do was get some water. So I stumbled to the kitchen knocking things over and bouncing off the walls. I knocked over a step ladder and knocked my work bag off the center island in the kitchen. I was completely out of it. After the drink I had this overwhelming feeling that I was going to have an

accident in my pants so I stumbled back to the bedroom then to the bathroom. The craziest thing was that I was sweating so bad that I left a puddle of sweat in front of the toilet. As I was sitting there my whole body starting to tingle like your foot or hand would if you cut off the blood flow for a minute or so. About 15 minutes after the initial cramp I was totally fine. I did not tell Lya about this event for a while. I did not want her to get worried with me spending many nights in Denver by myself. I honestly thought that it happened because I got out of bed to fast and got light headed and then my body just went into shock. It was very scary though.

The second time it happened was when I was working three jobs and coaching football. I was taking a nap around 2pm at home and Lya called my middle son Jeffery to make sure I got up in time to make it to practice. Jeffery came in and woke me up and as I got up my inner thigh began to cramp. I did not think anything thing of it at first, just stood up and stretched to get the cramp out. At that point I started to get light headed and all I wanted was a drink of water. I was leaning on my dresser so I turned around and grabbed my water bottle. After a quick drink I realized that I had to go to the bathroom once again just like before. I was yelling for help because I knew that Jeffery was home and I thought Lya was as well. Because I was working so much and sleeping very little, we had shut the door to the bedroom and had an industrial fan going so it would drown out any noise and I could sleep. Problem is, no one could hear me yelling. As I was trying to get to the bedroom door I fell to the floor, fractured my thumb as I broke a cloths hamper, and hit my head on dresser. I laid there for a minute once again sweating so bad that my clothes were soaked and the carpet was wet. I was doing everything I could to keep the cramp out and get the door open so I could get to the bathroom.

I finally crawled far enough to get the door open and had to drag myself out of the bedroom to have my son Jeffery help me. Jeffery was sitting on the couch and came running over to help me. He was scared because he could see how bad I was sweating and he said I was white as a ghost. Jeffery helped me stand up and I made it to the bathroom barely. Same situation as I was sitting there, I got all tingly and after a few minutes I felt completely fine except my thumb and head. I immediately remembered what had happened to me in Denver a few months earlier and it was exactly the same pattern. I was pretty confident it was related to my leg cramp. The next day I went to the ER for my thumb. While I was there the doctor explained to me about my femoral artery being cut off from the cramp, it was very scary to say the least.

The third time it happened Lya was sleeping and I was

watching a show. I reached down to scratch the bottom of my foot and felt the cramp coming on. I jumped out of bed yelled to Lya for help and headed straight into the bathroom before I began to black out. I ran in there because I wanted to stand in front of the mirror and watch what my body was going through, plus based on last two times I would need to use the bathroom anyway. I was standing in front of the mirror leaning on the counter and stretching my leg to try and keep the cramp out or at least minimize how severe it would be. I asked Lya to get my water bottle from the bedroom, I was so thirsty. At that point I was still lucid, by the time she got back in the bathroom I was out of it. Lya told me I was pale white and slurring my speech to her. I just knew I needed a drink and had to get to the toilet. Lya helped me to the toilet and once again as I sat there I was sweating through my cloths, a few minutes later got the tingles, and then was fine.

When I was with the doctor after the second episode I told her about the things that happened each time. First this overwhelming thirst! Second the need to go to the bathroom and empting my system out. Third the profuse sweating followed by the whole body tingling. The doctor explained to me that my body was going into protection mode to protect my heart and brain due to the restricted blood flow. That is why it was flushing anything it did not need to live. Needless to say, I stay very aware of the soreness in my inner thigh area and do everything I can not to get a cramp in that area. Even with that I make no excuses, I still walk every day. The Price is worth the Price!

Chapter 4

"Show me the little things you are doing today. I will show you the impact you will have later!" Pastor Dave McCabe

Painting the picture of what the first six months of getting my life back looked like. Please remember that for the entire 6 months and the 2 years that followed I worked at Jack in the Box, and traveled on a regular basis. I will tell you up front working in the fast food industry for 20 years was not the reason for my obesity! 100% of my obesity was me, my fight, my habits and behavior's. I would have gotten that big whether I worked in food, was a teacher, or worked in a hospital. My journey shows that even when working in the food industry and eating two, three and sometimes five times a day at fast food, if you make the right decisions about food, and stay active, you can make it.

Side bar: I recently was employed at an amazing hospital, but I can honestly say I was shocked at the amount of overweight and obese people who worked in the hospital. In my opinion no one sees the negative effects of obesity more than a hospital employee especially the incredible nurses who care for the patients. To me this was Gods way of confirming what my path in life has to be. If the very people who passionately care for those suffering from obesity and obesity related diseases struggle with weight themselves, we have a fight on our hands!

Back to the first 6 months, as I shared previously I walked 1 mile in 41 minutes on the first day. It was brutal, but on day two I did it again. Because I was a salaried manager in the food industry, I worked a lot of hours. Day seven was my first day off. I decided to walk to the bottom of Prune Hill. It was a half mile to the school then from the school to the bottom of Lake Road was 2.4 miles down hill with some steep decline. So going down was all good! I get to the bottom then walked on Heritage trail until the two mile marker and turned around. Here is the picture, I had been walking for six days in a row no more than three miles at a time, with some intermittent inclines and I had lost 11 pounds so I was down to 324 pounds. I got back to the bottom of Lake Road at the park and realized I had over two miles of uphill walking to do to get home and there was no way I was going to call for a ride.

To give you an example of the incline, over the last 3.5 years I have walked thousands of miles, hiked the foothills of the Rockies daily, climbed Multnomah Falls and Larch Mountain twice, and went on countless hikes with the family. I am in the best shape of my life and there is two different stretches on the climb up Lake Road and Everett Street that the incline still kicks my tail when I walk them.

Bottom line I made it home. Not without pain, cramping, and little bit of self talk. The kind where you question you own sanity! Recap of day seven over 10 miles walked in a little over 4 hours.

That began a pattern of at least once a week I would walk to the bottom of prune hill walk around Camas then walk home. To say I was obsessed would be a true statement. For once I had a plan that was simple, duplicatable, and gave me results. I walked to save my life!

Chapter 5

"Big things are achieved through the culmination of little things done right" Pastor Dave McCabe

The first six months definitely had challenges. I worked a lot of hours at a very tempting job for a food lover. I traveled at least one time in all six months for work. For me travel has always been a time about eating great food and fellowship with peers and friends. Plus when I traveled for work the boss's always took the group for dinner every night. Dinner was always at nice places with incredible food. I got to the point where I would look up the menu online to plan my meals and then I would input the food into my BodyBugg, this way I knew my calories for the dinner before I went to eat. This behavior did not happen overnight, I had to learn this. Remember the Prize never changed (healthy life) but the Price got adjusted along the way.

There were many trial and errors, but every day I walked. Breakfast was typically a buffet at the hotel, and lunch was catered to the meetings buffet style. We always had cookies and soda available for snacks. Sometimes I wonder how I made it. Oh yeah the Prize became big enough! When traveling for work I would typically get up two hours before breakfast time and walk for at least an hour to an hour and a half then get ready for day. I loved the trips to San Diego and Pleasanton because I could walk outside. Boise and Seattle trips in the winter I hit the hotel gym. Each night when the group would get together for some unwind time, I went to the treadmill to unwind. It helped me resist the temptation of late night fried food snacking. For some reason chicken wings, cheese sticks, and nachos at the hotel bar are much better after 10pm! I had to eliminate the temptation, besides I do not drink alcohol so that temptation was never there.

As I mentioned, I coach high school football and every spring we go to a team football camp for four days. This was my first year of coaching at Camas High School were my oldest son Joey was an incoming freshman. In June we go to Oregon State University for football camp. I have been going to camp for 18 years and the one thing they do is feed you well! The camps typically have 500 high school boys so you know there is a lot of food and they feed you buffet style with multiple choices three meals a day. Every kid brings extra food. I have been taking my three sons to camp with me since there were out of diapers. I always took extra snacks for them, and there was never a shortage of food. So I was a solid four months into my walking, but the temptation of readily accessible food was a tough mental battle.

The way I had learned to fight the temptations was to

walk extra. Any downtime I would walk. The cafeteria where meals were served had posted hours of operations. I would walk until it was the last twenty minutes they were open. I would then go get my meal, still making smart decisions, eliminating the temptation to over eat. By now I had come too far and the Prize was in sight. I was exactly where I needed to be in to lose 100 pounds in six months. I became relentless in my Price! I walked every morning before any kids were up, walked at lunch, and dinner. By this time I was walking a minimum of eight miles a day at an average of 3.8 mph. With my extra walking and coaching at camp I typically got in 35000 steps a day an average of 18 plus miles walked during the week of Football camp.

The next challenge I faced in first six months, was the Fourth of July week. My father in law Larry is a pyro-technician, so the whole family camps for about a week and helps with the set up and the show on the 4th. I love to travel and go on vacation for food and fellowship. This is a behavior that I still work on to this day and will for rest of my life. There are typically 15 to 20 family members camping so there is always big meals and extra food around. I can honestly say this was the toughest week for me.

There were no distractions of work or coaching football just family, food and free time. Not to mention my in laws Larry and Sue are phenomenal cooks! Sue makes the best elephant ears with homemade frosting when camping, funnel cake with powdered sugar, and smore's every night around the camp fire. It was walking talking sea of food temptation! One of the greatest victories of the first six months for me is that the week of the 4th of July I lost five pounds. I passed a major hurdle that week and I was a month away from my six month weigh in. I was slightly ahead of the pace I needed to be at to lose 100 pounds. But I was so scared of giving in even just a little that I did not want to say to myself "it is ok I can make it up later." I knew that the focus for six months would save my life.

I would get up each morning at 5 am, get dressed in the car so not to wake the family up in the tent, and I would walk on the highway leading up to Mount St Helen's. We were camping at Silver Lake Resort so I would use the mile markers on the highway and walk five miles away from camp, turn around and come back to camp. 10 miles minimum each morning before most were awake. The Prize was worth the Price! I would also walk with the family at different times throughout the day. We would go for hikes and just stay active as much as possible. Oh by the way no elephant ears, funnel cake, or smore's on the camping trip because the price was not worth it.

You see one of the things I have learned is that the short focused 6 months of discipline "the price" has changed and saved my life. I will have an elephant ear now when camping but I will split it with my wife or one of the kids. I will only eat half of an elephant ear instead of two for breakfast. I used to take the left over elephant ears and hide them in our tent and snack on them throughout the day. I was obsessed when it came to food. Would I have had the strength and discipline like this if I had started my 6 month journey in June? I don't know. I like to think I could have, but the reality is I probably would have given in to some of the food temptations.

I would have still walked but I would have been having the mental battles of guilt from the food I had eaten and who knows where it would have lead. It was God's plan for me and my journey to start when I did in February and place the temptations in life when he did. I averaged eating a minimum 5000 calories a day before I started walking

not including soda. I had some incredibly bad habits to

overcome.

Chapter 6

"What your mind can conceive you can achieve!" John Maxwell

I make it through the travel, football camp, 4th of July week and now I am on the home stretch of the 6 months to lose 100 pounds. Really the last 4 weeks were a blur. I stayed very focused and I was slightly ahead of my goal at each weekly weigh in so all was good. By the way, weighing yourself daily can play major games with your mind and I would strongly discourage it! I did it for years, not sure why. I think I was hoping some miracle would happen and I would lose 10 pounds when sleeping! Funny thing, it never worked though. The body is a crazy thing and water can fluctuate daily and change the numbers up or down. Stick to once a week as much as possible. I admit I still will weigh myself everyday at times then I get all crazy in the head.

If you are honest with yourself and create the behaviors and habits of eating better, moving more, and being consistent with it you will lose weight. I had a few weeks where I would work my tail off, eat amazing, and have a half a pound weight loss. Instead of getting frustrated at the result, I learned to focus on the behavior's I was putting in. The next week I would lose 7 or 8 pounds. I don't have the answer for why it was that way, everyone's body is different. I just know the repeated behaviors (the Price) lead to incredible results (the Prize). I am in no way an expert and there are so many people who are way more educated and knowledgeable on weight loss and the body then I am. I just know that I ate less and better, walked a lot, burnt more calories than I ate everyday for 6 straight months, and lost 101 pounds. I stuck to the plan for 12 months and lost 140 pounds, and I sit here now in the lobby of 24 hour fitness after a workout and rehabbing from my shoulder surgery still down 146 pounds almost 4 years later. All because I went for a walk one day and have not stopped walking since.

My six month weigh in day was August 10, 2010. On the 7th of August I drove a route from my house that was 13.1 miles because I wanted to walk a marathon before my weigh in. I had walked some 20 plus mile days before but they were split up in 2 or 3 different walks throughout the day. By this time in my journey my morning walk was at minimum of 10 miles round trip. I had the perfect route as we had moved from Prune Hill and bought some property in the Fern Prairie area of Camas. From my front door to the park at Lacamas Lake is 3.4 miles and there is a bathroom there, a major bonus as hiding behind trees can be a lot of work. From that point I could walk heritage trail which is 3.5 miles from the bathroom on one end to the bathroom on the other end. Or I could climb Lake Road drop down Payne Rd walk by Camas Meadows golf course, and end at the west end of Heritage Trail, again, at the bathroom. Noticed a trend yet? I planned my walk by way of a bathroom. I would then walk another 3.1 miles from Heritage Trail to my front door. I know it might sound crazy that I know the mileage in that detail but I set daily goals and was relentless to meet or exceed those goals. I would drive my routes and set mileage landmarks so I knew if I deviated from my paths, how long it would take and what my mileage would be. I typically worked 60 plus hours a week not counting football, so time was important for me. Now I just use an app on my phone and GPS tracks everything for me. It even shows me my mph, average minutes per mile, and a map of where I walked. You've got to love technology. I am sitting at the gym now writing my story on a Kindle Fire.

Back to my marathon, I had no clue how long it would take to walk a marathon I knew what it felt like to walk at 4.5 mph pace for a couple hours straight so I set the goal to walk the marathon in 6.5 hours that would be about a 4.2 mph pace. Remember I am competitive so I had to have a target to shoot for. I get up at 5 am on August 8 load up my hiking pack and off I go. I had not considered the extra weight of my hiking pack, full of extra food and water. There was an extra 6 to 8 pounds of weight not planned for, plus the back pack is twice the size of my usual camel pack. I typically carried one bottle of water and one snack in my camel pack for my daily walks. It did not matter, I had a goal; First to finish the 26.2 miles, second to see how fast I could do it. I left my house at exactly 6am on the 8th and walked back in the front door at 12:47pm! With a fifteen minute break in the middle, 6 hours and 32 minutes for a marathon, I was excited! To me it was a validation of all the hard work so far that I had put in. I went to dinner that night with my wife and enjoyed whatever I wanted just not out of control. I had weighed myself before the marathon and was already at my 100 pound mark, so I was smart in my dinner. On the 9th of August I went back to my routine normal walk, tracking my food, in putting it in the BodyBugg system, and getting ready for 6 month weigh in the next day.

August 10th 2010 comes step on the scale 101.3 pounds smaller than I was 6 months earlier, and 130 pounds smaller then the picture taken in San Francisco 8 months earlier. It was awesome to achieve, but by that time it was a habit and I was not done. A lot of things mentally changed for me over those 6 months. I still walked for me and my health, but also realized I walked for others as well. The feedback and encouragement I received from others was amazing. I did not realize God sent me on that dreadful first mile on February 10th to not only save my own life but to impact so many others.

Chapter 7

"Set out to gain life not lose weight!" Trey Bonner

I will share some of the lifelong behaviors and challenges with food I had to overcome in the first 6 months. As I shared earlier food was a learning process for me. I set my daily goal at 1950 calories. I was not sure what that looked like or even if it was a good goal. I just remember every time I would see % of daily value it was based on 2000 calorie daily intake. One big help for me was that the BodyBugg program had a number of foods and details preprogrammed in. So I was able to do some pre work on meals. As time went on I got better and better at planning and preparing my food. In the beginning I pretty much ate the same things every day. I can be a creature of habit so in the beginning for me the easier the better. Plus I honestly did not trust myself with food. Not only did I make bad food choices, I always over ate.

Back in 2006 I scheduled a doctor appointment because I was so frustrated about my weight gain. I remember going to the Dr and weighing in at 338 pounds. I was so mad. So the doctor starts all the usual tests and questions. I remember telling the doctor that nothing had changed for me over the last 3 or 4 years to cause me to gain weight every year, or so I thought. I was eating just as much as I had been, and other than working on my feet 10 hours a day and coaching football, I had no physical activity. The day of my first visit they had me do a treadmill test to check my heart. I made it 4 minutes 13 seconds walking! I was exhausted and cramping up so bad I had to stop. I remember the time to the second because it was very humbling. Surprisingly and thankfully my heart was in very good shape. Two weeks after the first appointment I had my follow up to get all the blood results.

Most of them I already knew because I was having my blood tested a minimum of once a month trying to pinpoint the cause of my cramping. So I meet with the doctor and he reviews my treadmill test which looks very good, my blood sugar is amazing-not even pre diabetic, cholesterol was perfect, and all other tests came back as normal. So the doctor looked at me and I quote you his exact words. "Dale based on your tests you are in great health! You are just fat!" I did not take any offense to this because I had been with this doctor for a while, I was comfortable with him, and we had a good and honest doctor/patient relationship. He was blunt and that's what I relate to. Now we were talking about next steps and he said something to me that at that time did not hit home with the impact it does today. The doctor told me just to maintain my current weight of 338 pounds I had to be in taking at minimum 6000 to 8000 calories a day and that if I was gaining weight I was eating more than that! This appointment was in early November of 2006 and I knew I had to do something about it (after the holidays). January 2007 new year's resolution! By the end of February 2007 I was done with it, the Price was too hard! The Prize was not big enough.

Funny little side note, among the many tests for my cramping and the 2 muscle biopsies my doctor ordered an MRI of my spine. Apparently there is a disease in the spine that can cause muscle cramping. About a week after my MRI I receive an alarming call from the nurse at my neurologist office. She tells me to call the Kaiser hospital in Portland to order a "Stat" CT scan on my head and neck. This freaks me out, I have watched enough TV to know "Stat" means urgent! So I ask the nurse what is going on what did the MRI find. She was very vague but she did tell me they found numerous enlarged lymph nodes in my neck and they needed to get a better look at them. I have the CT scan then wait for an appointment to open with an ear nose and throat specialist. They were concerned I had cancer. At the first appt, our 12 year old son Joey was with us. We go through the battery of tests and questions and the doctor explains the surgery, what to expect after, and the wait time on results to see if lymph nodes are cancerous. I apologize! I said this would a funny little side note and while writing it none of it is very funny at all. It was actually the scariest thing I have ever been through. Married, single income, 3 young boys at home, I was 36 years old. There were lots of prayers lifted up during this trail in life. Now to the funny part; the specialist was the nicest young lady and at the end of the appointment she was trying to palpate my lymph nodes in my neck. About 5 minutes of trying to feel the size of the nodes she finally said "Mr. Rule I am having trouble finding the lymph nodes because you have a (after a short pause) very generous neck ". With my sense of humor I immediately jump in with "so generous is the nice way of saying fat?" the poor doctor was so embarrassed but I assured her I was not offended. Now my son got the biggest kick out of this comment and he told that story to everyone about my generous neck. All tests came negative and all follow up appointments have been negative.

Wow I get side tracked easily, now back to the first 6 months of eating. As I mentioned earlier my in laws are incredible cooks, we all live together, and we regularly eat dinner as a family at the table. It is such a blessing for my boys to have this opportunity in life. In the beginning I did not eat with the family, again, I did not trust myself and had a lot to learn and numerous habits and behavior's to change. Please don't feel you can't do what or how I did it this is just my story. No two stories will be the same.

Please create your story it will probably save someone's life!

Back to dinner I eventually began eating dinner at the table with the family when I was not at work. It was quite a scene at the table. I always sat at the end of the table so I would have my plate in front of me, a digital scale to the left of the plate, and my lap top to the right. I would weigh and input my food into the BodyBugg before I ate. I became my way of holding myself accountable. Remember I was breaking at least 25 years of bad food habits. Again this is just my story find what works best for you and stick to it until you hit your goal, not someone else's goal or plan. Get a structure and an outline and then operate within that outline. After all it's your life you are saving. It has to be your plan that you will carry on the rest of your life, in my personal opinion!

The first block of my foundation is to go for a walk. I

still struggle with size of bites and speed I eat at. I pretty much ate anything I wanted during the six months but I did eliminate fried food and sweets and minimized my bread and pasta. I minimized those because of the amount of calories in each serving. I wanted to still be able to eat food so I would eat the foods that were lower in calories. That way I could have more throughout the day. Most people are surprised to hear I ate potatoes almost every day and still lost the 100 pounds in six months. I found that it's not the potato, but how it's cooked and what is put on the potato that buries you in calories. One big key for me is that I don't drink calories. Those calories I like to call the invisible calories because they are consumed so fast. Out of sight out of mind! As I shared before, I would drink almost as many calories a day in soda as I ate. Those were all empty calories with no value to my body what so ever. Still to this day 99% of what I drink has zero calories. I drink water nonstop and I don't drink soda, beer, or alcohol. I will occasionally have a sports drink or energy drink. I do have a 5 Hour Energy before my daily walk. A little caffeine to start the day, never have been a coffee or tea drinker.

In the first 6 months I had a lot to learn and 4 years later I am still learning! I was relentless in changing habits for those 6 months through a lot of trial and error. Those basic behavior changes made over 6 months saved my life and have given me a foundation to build on. I definitely still have meals that I struggle not to over eat. My goal is that if I have a tough meal not to allow it to become a tough day of meals. When it comes to food I have adopted the "everything in moderation" motto. The ability to have one or two bites of cake, pie, and ice cream has had a huge impact on my life. I am no way even close to perfect with food! That is another reason I walk everyday as a reminder of where I was and never want to be again.

A little trick I have learned on holidays and family event days I will walk extra sometimes an extra 8 to 10 miles in the morning even it is a work day I will just wake up a couple hours earlier and go. That is me now 4 years later, in the beginning it was an extra mile or two on those days. Another tip that has really helped me is I try to walk at least 1 mile after dinner more if time permits. This is great for the metabolism of dinner and keeps the calories burning when sleeping. Interesting side note at least for me; as I have been writing this last 30 minutes or so, I have been walking in circles around the basketball court at 24 hour fitness using my Kindle and dodging basketball's, workout equipment, a trainer and his client, and players. The majority of my story is being written while riding on a stationary bike, I might as well be burning some calories!

Bottom line for me with food is this I had to learn to

control food and not allow food to control me. "Energy Flow's were the Attention Goes" The battle with this is if you don't eat you will die and if you over eat it you will die. What you eat will impact the quality of your health while you are alive. Here is the victory! You can beat it I promise you, because I did, one step at a time literally. I tell people all the time walking was my gateway to saving my life. It is something I can do everyday even after walking a marathon, or walking 91.3 miles in 24 hours, or averaging 33,000 steps a day for 71 consecutive days. Truth is 99% of people can walk even if it is with the aid of a walker or cane. Remember the first day February 10, 2010 when one mile took me 41 minutes, but I never stopped walking day after day and here I am four years later on my light days I walk four miles and normal days are 8 to 15 miles days. You can do it if you make the Prize (living a healthy life) big enough and are will to pay the

Price determined by you and supported by others.

Chapter 8

"What you lift up in life will become the important things in life!" Pastor Dave McCabe

Life is full of twists and turns and can quickly derail you without a plan in place. Shortly after my 6 month weigh in my life was put in a potential crossroad. During an area ride with my director of operations at Jack in the Box I was asked what my future thoughts were about staying with the company. This did not come as a big surprise to me or my friend Jeff Tennant, another district manager who was on the ride with us. We knew that the areas we were in charge of were for sale and soon to be franchised. Jack in the Box is a great company! I worked for phenomenal leaders who were very invested in my growth as a person and a leader.

As a young leader I had a lot to learn. I was a very driven manager and as I shared I am very competitive. I was very blessed to be a high performer in results. Early on I would muscle the results and work long hours so my overall performance would not suffer when was not there. I was willing to pay the Price at work to get the Prize of recognition and more money. Many times as a manager this backfired as I was often viewed as cocky and a screwball among my peers, I love to have fun, but when it came to performance I struggled to understand why other managers could not get results. In my mind results were the easy part, developing people is where the real the work was.

As a manager I eventually learned to spend all my time invested in and developing my people. A valuable lesson learned from coaching football, and years of trying to muscle my results at work. Even as a manager at 23, I understood those basics because I had already been coaching football for 5 years. Now I needed to learn how to apply them to people. Little did I know God was already at work developing me to become a leader and a developer of leaders not just a manager. I was learning those behaviors many times the hard way. I was creating a self discipline that would later show up in the way walking saved my life. Also that passion created for the success of others still inspires me to walk, write my story, and grow my nonprofit to have an impact on this world.

Here is an example of me having to learn the hard way. At 25 I was fired from a very good paying job that I was a top five performer at, with two young children at home and my amazing wife was a stay at home mom. I was fired because I did not feel my raise was big enough and my response was one of emotion. I said things to my boss and his boss that were not appropriate. I was selfish, cocky, and self entitled because I felt disrespected based on where my performance was. I had a lot to learn in life! 6 months after being terminated from Taco Bell my life began to change by starting my career at Jack in the Box. It was not always rose's, but eventually I got out of my own way and had some incredible mentors step into my life and tell me the truth. Interestingly enough that drive I had for performance transitioned into a drive to develop others.

Then I finally took that passion for others, looked in the mirror, and applied it to my own life. I finally realized if I am to do what God has planned for me, which is to have an impact on others, I actually had to be alive to do it! I can honestly say 100% of the success I ever achieved at work sits squarely on the crew members, team leaders, assistant managers, and restaurant managers who trusted this crazy passionate guy. Chris Crouch, Fred Bergeron, Maria Hollandsworth, Shelly Rholfs, Alison Layfield,

Christina Camara, Loni Hobson, Deb Sandin, Jeff Tennant, Shanna Kilpatrick, Debbie McNally, Shelley Uhrman, and many I have missed I could never repay you for what you have poured into my life impacting me even when you did not know it. Lenny Comma you inspire me, you challenge and motivate me to be more than I think I can be. Your passion and belief stretch me even when we talk only once a year. I am a better person because you are my friend, honest, bold, and empowering!

Chapter 9

"It's easy to point, it's hard to examine!" Pastor Dave McCabe

The date today is 12/12/2013 and I will share with you the last four and a half weeks of my life. A life very similar to what we all go through especially in the battle against weight. I have been recovering from shoulder surgery for 6 months and during that time things have been pretty good but I have noticed myself off and on struggling with my food. Since my last 24 hour walk on Sept 6 2013 when my weight was at 225 pounds I have slowly put on weight. About 10 pounds until four weeks ago and in the last four weeks I put on 17 pounds! Today is my personal wake up call. I honestly did not see this coming but all the sudden I found myself sneaking to the store to buy food from the deli and eating it in the car so my wife would not know. My wife and children have been my priority for a long time and we were blessed for many years financially were she did not have to work and was able to stay home and raise our three sons.

We made a significant financial decision 3 years ago when my only options at Jack in the Box was to move or leave the company. We decided as a family not to move. I have been asked several times why did I leave a great job that I was growing at and had great potential at. The answer is always the same. I have one chance to raise my children, and I have my whole life to make money. My boys have gone to the same school their whole life and my oldest Joe was entering his sophomore year at Camas High School. My other boy's Jeff was going into 7th and Josh into 6th. They have friendships that will last a lifetime and I felt it was very important to keep those things in place rather than chase money.

So I spent some time searching and looking for where I would work and at one point I was working 4 jobs including coaching football. When I injured my shoulder at one of my jobs it impacted my ability to work any of them so our income once again took a hit. For me one of the many blessings of my wife staying home is that after being diagnosed with M.S. about 7 years ago she could avoid the extra stress of working. Not that she could not work, but she did not have to. I loved the opportunity to provide for her and the boys. Now my amazing wife works 3 jobs as I recover. I knew that this bothered me but did not know how much until recently.

My wife loves what she does she is a preschool teacher at a Christian school, a home care provider, and she cleans our church 4 days a week. She works about 60 hours a week. Some may think it's my pride talking, but the reality is that it is my responsibility to provide for my family, and that inability has had an impact on me. I went from working 2 to 3 jobs, playing with my kids, and lifting weights to not working, could not lift weights, play basketball, or throw a football. Just about everything came to a sudden stop with the injury, except walking which has kept my mind sane. I honestly believe I was depressed and definitely afraid that this injury was going to change my life. I had lost sight for about a month or so of the PRIZE.

I just continued to pray and fight, that is all I know how to do. I used to just fight and sometimes pray. Now I pray first then keep fighting. As I reflect it is amazing how quickly an addiction like I have to food can overtake your life, even though I have been so engaged in the battle of obesity for three plus years. That is why I shared this battle with you. There will be battles to fight. Times you slip up and have adversity in life. You and I need the PRIZE of living healthy to be present and aware at all times. We all need a support structure. Mine is my faith first, my family second, and my close friends third. To grow and change you have to all allow yourself to be vulnerable and humble. So those who are willing to help feel empowered to help. I have learned part of the PRICE is being vulnerable enough to admit to failing so I can grow.

Chapter 10

"Surround yourself with people who build you up not beat you up!" Dale Rule

I am just here to tell you my story not to preach or influence on faith, but the most important part of my story is my walk with Jesus. You don't have to be a believer! That is called free will. Free will is a gift from God. But I challenge you to be an investigator! Make an informed and educated decision on your beliefs.

Now it is the middle January 2014 and I wrote last month that I was dealing with some things in my life and that maybe I was a little depressed. I believed at the time that it was my wake up call. I was wrong! I had not hit rock bottom yet. Over the next five weeks I struggled to get out of bed. I would get up each morning to take my oldest son to school then go back to bed. If I had a DR appointment or therapy for my shoulder I would go, then go back to bed. I would then pick up my youngest son from middle school and take him to the high school to lift with the football team. I would stay at the high school for one and a half hours do my shoulder rehab, walk on the treadmill, then go home and go back to bed. I was spending close to 20 hours a day in bed. I was depressed. I was at rock bottom. Thank you Jesus for the last three plus years of my life with walking, and all the relationships that has come from it. I am afraid to think of where I would be today without it.

I can say the last two and a half months have mentally been the hardest of my life. Walking has strengthened my faith. There is no way I could have done the things I have done without my relationship with Jesus, my Lord and Savior. I have walked so many miles by myself it has given me so much time to pray and reflect on my life, what God has already done, were he is still working and taking me. My marriage is stronger and incredible people have been placed in my life. Goals and vision far beyond what I can accomplish on my own all because one day I went for a walk to save my life. Walking saved my sanity over the last couple of months.

God pulled me up by the people he has placed in my life. First is my amazing wife Lya who never judged me when I was at my lowest. Lya is always supportive and most important praying. My Mom who always listens, then worries, then prays for me. Mike Mihaljcic a former player and lifelong friend, thanks for listening. John Blair, your encouraging words and empowering attitude even when you did not know what I was going through. Matt Lang, our amazing youth Pastor at Grace Foursquare, calling me out when you ask me how I was doing and I would lie and say I was doing great. You have the heart and willingness to see through it and then lift me up with your words and love. So many others who had a kind word for me in those rough months. You lifted me without even knowing it.

Don Lovell you changed my life, first your selfless attitude towards me and others, then your incredible enthusiasm for me and my story. I am embarrassed to admit it but during those two and a half months I was too ashamed to call you, my mind and self worth was taking a beating. Finally I called and asked you to lunch and that day and the following 10 days re energized me. First you did not judge what I was going through. You were empathetic and encouraging, but most important you were brutally honest! The only way I could ever repay you is to finish what I started. I can honestly say you are the one who finally pushed me over the edge to write this book. Many people have heard my story and told me I should write a book, but you told me I had to write a book! Your enthusiasm and encouragement is amazing.

The second thing you did is introduce me to Alter Wiener, and that incredibly humble, kindhearted, selfless man changed the way I will forever think about other people. Once again Gods grace is written all over this journey. It is amazing how God will place people in our lives at times when we think we know why, and the truth is there is a much bigger plan for the people he places there. Don Lovell you were my Guardian Angel that day at lunch, thank you for allowing me to be vulnerable to you.

Chapter 11

"Courage is the ability to rise again when you have fallen! Humility is the ability to admit you fell and reach for guidance!" Dale Rule

When Don first told me about Alter and his story as a Holocaust survivor I was very interested to learn more, but I guess I was not ready in my life to hear it. Don first told me about Alter and his story in October 2013. I had recently finished my 3rd 24 Hour Walk and my body was still beat up. We were a little over half way done with the football season and I was busy with shoulder rehab. I also did not realize I was headed for such a trying time in my life dealing with self doubt and depression. Even with all this going on I would still think about the story Don had told me about Alters life. On a couple of occasions I had looked through my notes because I thought I had written down Alters name and the name of his book. I never found it, I was not ready to receive Alters message for my life. Now it's January 2014 and Don and I are at lunch. I ask Don what was the Holocaust survivors name and the name of his book? I was at a place in my life were I needed to read the book, but I did not know that at the time.

It seems to be all about Gods timing when some things will have the greatest impact on you. Sometimes when we get the message when we are not ready to receive it, we get motivated for a quick minute instead of impacted for life. I believe if I had read Alters book in October it would not have had the same impact on the rest of my life. Don reminds me of Alters name and the name of his book "From a Name to a Number". This time I put the info in my phone so I would not lose it.

I am not going to tell you Alters story, I could never do

it justice. Since you are reading this then odds are you are reading my book. I thank you for that from the bottom of my heart, but more importantly I ask please read "From a Name to a Number". When Lya got home from work that evening after I had lunch with Don, she downloaded the book for me. For the next 2 days I could not put it down. I finished it in 2 days which for me is an accomplishment. Alters book brought me hope in myself again. When I read Alters book I was at my lowest point in my 41 years on this earth. To read a story with such incredible tragedy and have a man come out of it with such a kind and forgiving heart, it brought me hope, focus, and perspective once again. In 2 days time I was reinvigorated to continue my journey. 5 days after reading the book I went to see Alter speak at David Douglas high school in Portland Oregon. It was impactful to see about 500 high school students completely focused for over an hour on this 87 year old man with broken English. No kids were talking or messing around and many of them had tears in their eyes throughout different parts of the presentation. It was incredible I can only hope to be blessed enough to have half the impact on people as Alter has and will have. I talked with Alter briefly before and after the presentation as Don had already informed Alter I was coming.

Three days later one of the fondest memories of my 41 years on this earth happened as Don and I drove to Alters apartment in Hillsboro Oregon to visit with Alter. It was a blessing, very challenging and uplifting. Don had already talked to Alter about my story and told him that I was writing a book about my walking and weight lose journey. So as we were all talking Alter wanted to hear my story, which compared to his is tiny. Alter was very encouraging and helpful and he challenged me to finish my book and even offered to help get it published if needed. Again I ask you, please read Alters book "From a Name to a Number" it might just change your life!

One week later my 3 teenage boys and I drove a little over an hour to see Alter tell his story. I could not wait for my boys to hear his story and get to meet him after. They could not stop talking about Alter and his story all the way home. They were impacted for life. One of the reasons I share meeting with you is that Alter asked me two questions. Two questions that I now know I needed to answer for myself and share with you as well.

2003

2004 Lya and I

2004   Lya and I

Watch my amazing wife's transformation as well no excuses even with being diagnosed with Multiple Sclerosis, absolute warrior!

2004

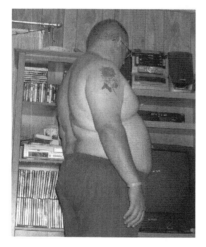

2005

2005 Lya and I

2005 Me and the Boys

2006 Jeffery and I

2006 Nephew Shane and I

2007

2008   2008

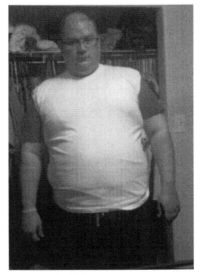

2008

2009 The Boys and I

2009 The Boys and I

2009   The Family

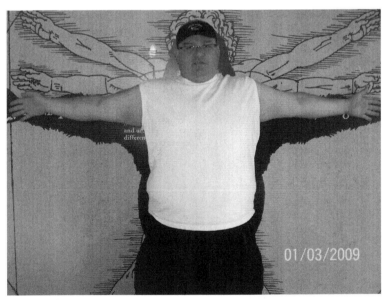

2009 that's a full size Gorilla (dark shadow) behind me

2009

2009

12/14/2009

The picture that started the change 56 inch pants 3x sweatshirt (Filled out!)
Monday night game in San Francisco 4 days later at home in Camas WA
stepped on scale 363 pounds

6 days before first walk on Feb 10th 2010 weighed 335 pounds already down 28 pounds from picture in San Fran, but was already done with my new years resolution bad habits were already creeping back in. 2 days later talked with Gary at sea tac airport, changed my life!

30 days

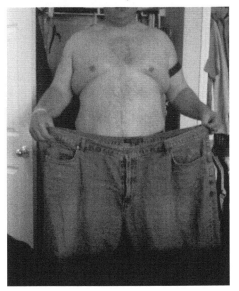

60 days

6 months 101.4 pounds lost, walking daily, eating less, no drugs, no diets, not one day in a gym. Just committed to burn more calories than I ate, relentless focus on daily getting my life back. No secrets, no fads, no miracles cures, no surgery, no $$$ (other than shoes), and I worked in the fast food industry. No Excuses!

Scale picture is 8 months after weighing in at 363 pounds 130 pounds down.

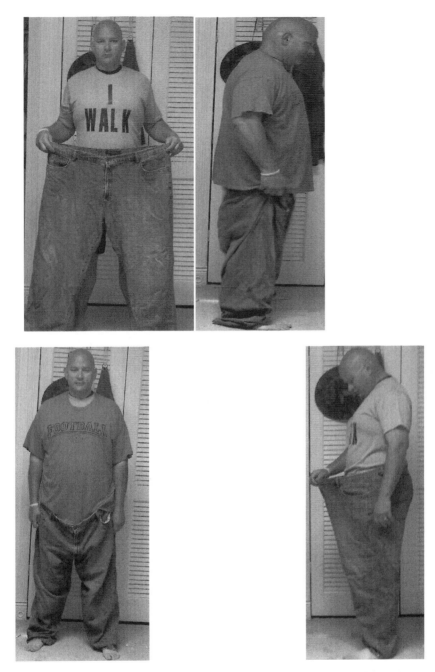

Same pants as seen in San Fran picture 56 in waist, 3x t shirt. 6 month pictures.

Walked in all weather conditions.

Same brand and style of shoe bought 4 months apart. Shoe on right worn out after approx 1200 miles of walking in 4 months

1 year weigh in from first walk Feb 2011 and 14 months from San Fran picture. Feb to Feb weight loss 335 to 219 12 months 116 lbs, 14 month weight loss 363 to 219 144 pounds WALKING!!

My oldest son Joey and I both in the pants from San Fran picture.

10 pairs of worn out shoes in the first year.

July 2011 still going strong, look at my amazing wife's transformation as well.

1st annual 24 hour walk for Obesity and M.S. awareness

Oct 2011, I was able to walk 71 miles in 24 hours.

Andrea and Dustin Krecklow

2nd annual walk for Obesity and M.S. awareness Sept 2012,

I was able to walk 79 miles in 24 hours.

Getting ready for Camas and Washougal Mayors weigh in for their completion.

Incredible seniors John Norcross, Troy Patterson

Washougal Mayor Sean Guard, Camas Mayor Scott Higgins

Bathroom and heater saving my life.

Jeff and Erika Tennant with their boys.

Pat and Connie Hennessey

Deb Sandin, Chad Schifman, Joe Driver, Me, Matt Clarkson

The tire tower

Finished

3rd annual walk for Obesity and M.S. Awareness and this year Testicular Cancer Sept 2013, I was able to walk 91 miles walked in 24 hours

Amazing wife Lya

Great shirt Scott Conlee!

Incredible Seniors leaders Dallin Bradshaw, Drew Clarkson, Taylor Kaufman, Michael Digenova, and Adam Dawson.

Many helping/pushing me to the end!

Difference maker Drew Clarkson on left sharing his survival from testicular cancer just a few months earlier. With Gage Clarkson and Josh Rule

Thank you ladies! with Camas mayor Scott Higgins and Reilly Hennessey

Pop Warner Team, Thank You Larry, Candi, John, Kris, and all the families and players for your belief in my passion.

Blazers dancers a huge hit! Thank you ladies for your commitment and time

Very Blessed former players form Centennial high Shane, Matt, and Zach, as well current players from Camas out in support.

Great leader and example John Eagle in red visor with his daughter Sophie, my niece Kayla Denham in hat and Reilly Hennessey

Matt Lang   A few of the Pop Warner boys

Mike Beasley and John Blair early morning hours

Inspirational Mayor Scott Higgins on his way to over 30 miles

Chapter 12

"Your history does not determine your Destiny!" Dale
Rule

After sharing my weight loss story and my upbringing with Alter the first question Alter asked me was "Dale are you bitter or angry about the way you were raised? Great question with an easy answer! No I am not one bit angry or bitter about my life. Alter asked me why I was not. I shared the following with Alter.

I have coached football in every social economic group from very poor to financially prosperous and everything in between. Dealing with so many differences in societies eyes I learned that I was suppose to fail. I learned I was a stereotype based on my upbringing. I was a poor inner city white kid from a broken single parent home. No male figure consistently in my upbringing, my mom on welfare and section 8 housing even though she worked full time. Statistically I was supposed to fail, but I did not know that. I only knew what I knew, that was my norm. More importantly God had bigger plans for my life.

We moved around a lot as I was growing up, sometimes for work, sometimes my mom chasing after my dad. 7th grade was the first full year of school that I completed start to finish at the one school after kindergarten. 1st through 8th grade I changed schools at least once every year except the 7th grade. I did complete all four years of high school at the same school, Madison High, in Portland Oregon. We lived in Northern California, Astoria Oregon, Reno Nevada, and South Central Oklahoma, before settling in Portland, Christmas of 1983. We lived in multiple little towns in California and

Oklahoma either on our own or with family. This was not abnormal to me this is what I knew so to me moving around was normal.

My mom Kathy has always been a hard worker often times working multiple jobs as I was growing up. My biological father Dale SR lived in Massachusetts where I was born and my Mom and Father separated when I was two. The last time I saw my Father was summer of 1984. My father had very progressive Multiple Sclerosis and passed away when I was in my mid 30's. As I look back I regret that I did not force the issue and build a relationship with my Father. When I was 4 my Mom married the man that has been my Dad for the last 38 years Chuck Miller.

Dad is a great man. I have learned many things from my Dad, both what to do and what not to do. Most of all I learned what unconditional love is. My dad and mom first split when I was 6. They had an off and on relationship for a few years after that which often involved Mom, my brother Darrel, and myself moving to where ever Dad was at the time. When I was 10 they finally split for good. Even though we were not his biological children and they were divorced, Dad was and still is our Dad. Always has been and always will be. To this day my Mom and Dad are friends and my Dads wife Joan is a second mother to me. Just to give you an example of the unconditional love they have for us, my Dad and Joan have been raising one of my brother's children Dalton for 6 years. Even though my Dad was not living real close to me throughout my middle school and parts of my high school years, I always knew I could count on him and Joan if needed.

I love my Mom, Dad, and Joan very much. They have always been behind me encouraging and supporting me. I come from what society labels a dysfunctional family, split home, biological father not in picture, and poor. When my

Dad married Joan my Mom and Joan became friends. My Mom was no threat to them and we were all a package deal. We have lived with my Dad and Joan on 2 different occasions. Myself, Mom, brother, Dad, Joan and Joan's 3 kids Darren, Ryan, and Heidi. To many this was dysfunctional, to me this was life. It was my normal and I knew nothing else.

I have watched my Mom battle mental health illness all my adult life and half the time I was in high school. Soon after I graduated high school my mom was admitted to O.H.S.U. in Portland on suicide watch. This was traumatic to me even though there were many times my Mom was not at home much, either working or playing she was the most consistent person in my life. At the time Mom was admitted I was a full time college student and working part time at a local fast food restaurant. We were on section 8 housing so they now covered all our rent, gave us an extra

$50 dollars a month, and we were already receiving food stamps. I tried to work as much as I could and go to school just to keep up on the bills, as well as deal with the unknown of whether my Mom was going to live or not. For about 4 months I honestly did not believe my Mom was going to live. It was traumatic to visit her and see her so despondent in life. I have to thank my girlfriend at that time Kim Payne. Kim was my rock and support at a very trying time in my young life. I had no clue what a roller coaster I was in for over the next 4 years. In and out of hospitals and clinics and many attempts to take her own life, it brings you some perspective in life.

Lya is amazingly patient and kindhearted! I would estimate my Mom has been with us for 90% of the time that we have lived together going on 19 years as I write today. Lya has such an incredible heart and love for others and trust me it was not always easy. We have recently moved my Mom into a Senior Active Living Community were Lya is her care giver.

I have learned great things from my Mom. Mom has a huge heart and passion to help others sometimes to her own detriment. She was always an incredibly hard worker and very loyal. Mom has always shown me unconditional love. My Mom is not without challenges but aren't we all. Being an observant learner I was blessed with the ability to learn both good and bad from watching others. Maybe this was my survival technique growing up? I call it a blessing and it worked.

I was surrounded by a lot of drinking and off and on drug use growing up, depending on which family members I was living with at the time. I am glad to say that I have never been much of a drinker other than about a 6 month stretch after high school when I and a few friends from school lived together. Even then I rarely drank. I am not against drinking, I just choose not to do it. I have personally seen some destructive behaviors that have been the results of drinking. I have smoked pot one time the summer before my senior year in high school on the 4th of July in Seaside Oregon.

My best friend growing up lived in Astoria at the time and I was working about 45 minutes from Astoria. I was bucking hay all summer to get ready for football and make school clothes money. My dad and Joan had a little farm in the middle of nowhere so I spent the summer with them. I went to Astoria to spend the 4th with Ralph and end up in Seaside with his younger sister Stacy to watch the fireworks. Stacy and I end up in her Mom Dee Dee's new car and smoke some pot before the fireworks start. After the fireworks I had to drive Stacy and I back to Astoria about 30 minutes away stoned, it was not fun. I went back to my Dads the next afternoon and I told him about that night. He asked me what I thought and I told him it was not worth it and have never touched it again.

I have never smoked cigarettes, been around smokers my entire life until I was about 25. I never had the desire or urge, probably taken 3 or 4 drags off a cigarette in my life to me it was nasty. The worst habit I had growing up was short lived. When I was in the 5th grade in Oklahoma I stared chewing because that what all the kids did, even the girls on our baseball team. My chewing habit was probably about 5 months long then came to a quick and traumatic end. One day we were playing basketball and I had a big chew in. While playing I got hit and swallowed every bit of chew in my mouth. I immediately started to vomit. I ran to my Mom's work and could not stop vomiting I thought I was going to die! Never touched it again!

I used to joke with people, I don't drink, smoke, or do

drugs because I already had one strike against me eating, and could not afford another. That's where my mind was around food and weight loss. I would joke to justify. When I was the wide receivers coach at Centennial I use to joke with the kids that my claim to fame was that I was the fattest, wide receiver coach in the state of Oregon! I was very accepting or avoiding of my weight issue. I could go on and on with different things I have seen or been part of growing up but I just wanted to give you a small glimpse into my upbringing and give you some history on how I answered Alters question. "Are you angry or bitter about your life or the way you were raised?" NO.

The circumstances of my upbringing does not define me it develops me. Through watching the success and failures of others I learned what to do and what not to do. I spent many lonely nights as a kid growing up terrified, scared of every noise. So I understand the importance of safety and feeling secure. I watched alcohol end marriages and in some cases end lives so I choose not to drink. I saw and see my Mom battle with mental illness, and to this day battle with thoughts self worth and suicidal thoughts. I do my best to be a lifter of people and not a leaner on people. I love my brother very much, but he has 5 children that do not have a Dad in their lives. I try to stay as active in my 3 boy's lives as possible.

We are not a victim of our circumstances. We are a victim of our reactions to our circumstances. Your history does not determine your destiny.

I have failed so many times and in so many ways but I refuse to stay down. I have learned so much because I am willing to fail that I could never be bitter or angry about my life. God has blessed me so much already. God gave me incredible examples both good and not so good to learn from. I am who am today because of the life I have had. I would not change one second of it or I would not be me. I love who I am and who I am becoming. It is encouraging to me to know that I am going to fail so many times but yet I am willing to fall so I can get up and grow. Courage is the ability to rise again when you have fallen. Humility is the ability to admit you fell and reach for and accept guidance.

Chapter 13

"You have to accomplish something mentally before you can physically!" Pastor Dave McCabe

The second question Alter asked me made me really dig deep and think. It was a very simple to the point question with a not so simple answer. Alter asked me in these exact words "Dale why were you so fat?" I immediately answered him with "because I love food"! Alter did not accept that answer and said to me "everyone loves food". Alter asked me again "Dale why were you so fat?" So I thought about it for a few minutes and I finally said to Alter "I do not have an answer for that question right now give me a little bit of time to think about it." Then Alter said if you want to have the impact you say you want, you have to be able to answer that question. You have to accomplish something mentally before you can physically. I had never really given much thought to why I ate so much and why I got so big. My first answer to Alter was the justification I have been using for years and that is that I love food, but Alter was right so does 99.9% of everyone else out there. So after about 20 minutes of thinking about it I had part of the answer for Alter.

One of the reasons I got so fat is that I know my mom loves me never have doubted it, but as I look back the #1 way my Mom has and does and to this day expresses her love is through food.

Another reason with being raised poor living on food stamps, powdered milk and free cheese from the government. I developed some bad habits around food. There was never a time where I did not clean my plate completely when eating. First off that was the rule at my grandpa's house when we lived there. Second of all there were times in middle and high school that by the middle of the month the only food I was guaranteed to have was free breakfast and lunch at school. This developed some mental habits that to this day I still have to be aware of. To get up from the table when there is still food at the table even when I have eaten plenty can be a mental struggle. I will convince myself I can eat more. At times I will use a small plate at the table so I can control this.

When we lived in Oklahoma much of the time my brother and I lived with our aunt and uncle. My aunt had very strict food rules. We were allowed three meals a day, and no snacks. She went so far as to put locks on the fridge, and cupboard doors. We lived with them off and on from 3rd to 6th grade. My brother is two years older than me. We took this as a challenge to always try and sneak food, and when we got caught which we often did the punishment was not pretty. The punishment always included a spanking, and almost always had the next meal taken away from us. Once again this created some bad habits that I would have to overcome. I became a food hoarder as I got older. Being unsure of whether or not you get a next meal either through punishment or not having food has a lasting impact.

I shared these with Alter but I knew there would be more things. I thought about triggers that I did not realize contribute to my eating habits. So after Don and I left Alters we were discussing all the things we had talked about and another thing popped into my head as we were pulling into Camas. When I got home I was sharing the evening with Lya and told her about the questions Alter asked me then I shared this next piece with her.

As I shared earlier I spent many nights growing up alone and scared especially after we moved to Oregon.

With my older brother out running the streets and my Mom either at work or at play I would turn to food for comfort. Many nights especially from the 8th grade on I would make the four portion size of instant mashed potatoes (they were cheap) with extra butter and if we had cheese or hamburger I would put it in grab a soda and head to bed. I would lay there in bed and eat, drink soda, and watch TV until I could not keep my eyes open. I would literally eat myself to sleep. Food became my security I would self sooth my fear and loneliness by eating.

Those are just a few examples of different habits/triggers that I have had to be aware of just like I shared earlier about travel and family functions they in the past for me were all about food.

When I was with Alter one of the things I shared with him were some of the habits I developed as a general manager and district manager in the food industry. The fast food industry is just that, fast, customers come in with the expectation to get their food hot and fast. So rarely did I take the time to eat properly. Typically I would eat in back of restaurant standing over the garbage can. Or I would snack all day while on the run. I would devour food in a couple of minutes, a habit I still struggle with today, I still eat too fast. Numerous times I would overeat because by the time my brain knew I was full I probably had doubled the amount of food I needed. I was usually in pain from eating so much. Today at the table I make an effort to put my fork down after each bite and do not pick it up until I have swallowed.

Many times as a general manager I would only eat twice a day while at work, but still consume more than 5000 to 8000 calories daily including soda. As a district manager I would typically eat 6 times a day at work, which is much better than twice a day depending on what and how much you ate. The problem was that each meal I was consuming was between 800 and 1200 calories including soda! That is 5000 calories on my low calorie day. All the food I was eating was from fast food and it was not the healthy options. I would eat at my restaurants typically three to four times a day and competitive shop at least one competitor restaurant a day sometimes two to three different competitors in one day. I had many 12000 to 15000 calorie days.

I was killing myself. I was an out of control food addict. I would keep cash on me on my days off just so I could go eat without my wife knowing. So in answer to Alters question, "How did I get so fat?" There are numerous reasons and yes I do love food, but after taking a hard look at my life, I realize that I self sooth fears and loneliness with food. I am emotional eater, and I can show my love and gratitude through food. I can be a food hoarder when times are tough. All triggers that I have to stay aware of when tempted.

Chapter 14

Building lives to touch lives!

I want to take a moment and share with you two people that have had a tremendous impact on my life. The first is a man that I honestly can say has had the biggest impact of the many men I have been so blessed to be influenced by. This man taught me how to be a father and a husband, interestingly enough at the time he did not even know it. As I shared earlier I am an observant learner. I love watching how people act and interact with others, that is how I learn. This in no way is meant to lessen the influence other men had on my life. When I was younger I had some great examples of husbands and fathers, but I was not in a place in life where I was ready or needed to learn from them. When I was 19 years old I got the opportunity to coach at Centennial high school in Gresham Oregon were I would coach for the next 16 years. God works in amazing ways! Chris Knudsen is the head coach at Centennial, and I had the privilege to work with, be mentored by, and watch Chris and his family for 16 years. When I started coaching Chris and Kathy's children Tyler and Brittany were very young I believe Tyler was in Kindergarten and Brittany was the youngest. I did not know at 19 years old God was placing Chris in my life to mentor me in much more than being a football coach. To watch how Chris and Kathy worked together first as a married couple then as parents was awesome. Chris I learned so much more than football from the example you were and still are today. Chris you are a hero to me. Thank you shaping this rowdy, loud, obnoxious 19 year olds life. Your footprints will forever be on my life!

The second person is Neva Miller who is no longer with us here on earth but is watching over every step I take from heaven. I first met Neva when we moved to Reno when I was 7. We moved around the Reno area for about two years before moving back to Chester Ca. then to Fletcher Ok. My mom and Neva were best friends and they stayed in touch over the years with Neva eventually moving to Portland Or. When I was 12 years old we were living in Oklahoma and my Mom came home one day and told my brother and I that the three of us were going to drive to California over Christmas break to see my Great Grandma then to Portland were we would be living with Neva and her daughter Cheri. Neva was an amazing lady who overcame many obstacles and adversities in her life. From battling morbid obesity to many health problems, Neva always had the best attitude and would help out anyone who needed it. We lived with Neva for one year then over the next seven years always lived within five blocks of where Neva lived. Neva was a second Mom to me. For all of my middle school and high school years, if I was struggling with life or tired of being scared and alone I went to Neva's. Neva loved my Mom but did not always agree with the choices she made. Neva always would help me when I needed help. I had went to church off and on growing up mostly with my Great Grandma when in California and then with friends in Oklahoma. Neva not only took me to church but Neva taught me about Jesus and the Bible. I gave my life to the God and accepted Jesus as my Lord and Savior through Neva's guidance. A gift I could never repay. Neva was there for me as well as Kim when my Mom had her mental breakdown. Neva was working with my Mom and is actually the one who drove my Mom to the hospital. Neva was always an ear to listen and knew what and when to give appropriate advice. Neva prayed for me continuously. Neva gave me advice on my marriage as Lya and I were starting our life together. Neva gave us advice as we became new parents. Neva was then and is now an Angel who has blessed my life in more ways than I could ever share in words. I miss Neva greatly but I know where she is and one day I will see her again. Neva was by far the most influential person in my life as I was growing up. I love you Neva thank you for everything.

Chapter 15

Ordinary people accomplish extraordinary things with extraordinary behaviors!

Back to my life after the first 6 months of walking; I want to take a few moments and share with you some of the things I have done walking. I did not know going for a walk was going to take my life were it has as I shared earlier I went for a walk in the beginning to save my life. Through me updating my results of walking, weight loss, and occasional pictures on Facebook I was getting incredible feedback and support. On May 1st 2011 I set a goal to take 30,000 steps a day for 30 consecutive days and posted it on Facebook. I had a pretty good idea what 30,000 steps a day looked and felt like, I had many days were I had already put in 30,000 steps since starting my walking journey in Feb 2010. So away I go putting in the miles and posting my steps each night. If had not posted my steps by late evening I would get friends and family asking me on Facebook where I was at for the day. It was awesome and held me accountable. I was still working 50 to 70 hours a week as a district manager for Jack in the Box, but now I was commuting from Camas Washington to Denver Colorado. I just made it happen, no excuses.

I want to share with you a few cool reactions from the weight loss. After accepting the position in Denver we had a meeting the 2nd day I was there. Lenny who I spoke about earlier was going to be attending the meeting. I had spoke to Lenny the previous December shortly after I had weighed myself at 363 pounds. We were having a holiday dinner in Portland for the leadership team. My boss at the time Maria liked to challenge me in a good way. So Maria decided to sit me in between the CEO of Jack in the box Linda Lang and Lenny who is the COO. Maybe Maria did this to make me behave at dinner? During dinner I was taking with Lenny who I trust and shared my frustration about my weight. I don't remember the conversation in detail, but Lenny did. Fast forward to the Denver meeting 12 months later; Lenny had heard that I had lost some weight, but we had not seen each other since the dinner in Portland. As Lenny was talking with the managers in Denver before the meeting, he was going to each of them and shaking their hands and introducing himself. As Lenny started to walk towards me I realized he did not recognize me. I was 140 pounds smaller then the last time I had seen him. Lenny walked up stuck out his hand and said "Hi I am Lenny" I shook Lenny's hand but did not say anything. At first he was kind of staring at me like "I know who this is but cannot place his name." I then said "Hi Lenny" and he immediately knew it was me by my voice. Lenny's reaction and words brought tears to my eyes. At first he was a little speechless then he told me how proud he was. It was then he reminded me of the conversation we had at dinner 12 months earlier. Lenny said to me that he had never heard that passion and commitment in my tone before. The way I was talking about having to change for myself and my family. He told me that he knew I could do it and more importantly that I would do it. Lenny was not surprised that I had lost weight, but was about the amount I lost in the amount of time I lost. I was very cool to see that reaction.

Another great moment is when I went over to my friend Matt's place. I hired Matt when he was 15 and have known him for many years. I had not seen Matt the entire six months of my weight loss. When I got to Matt's place he heard my voice so he knew I was there, but when he walked into the room I was in he did not know who I was until I spoke. Matt was amazed and very complimentary about what I was able to accomplish.

One last one, I coached football at Benson High the seasons of 2008 and 2009 and was over 350 pounds. In 2010 I had moved to Camas High were my son was an incoming freshmen. We had an evening practice in October 2010 and I was over in Portland so I decided to stop by Benson and say hi to the players and coaches. I had coached with the head coach Anthony for the last four years and many of the players were returning from the previous season. As I walked into practice not one coach or player recognized me. I was about 130 pounds smaller then the last time I had seen them. It was an awesome response I received from everyone once they realized who I was. Anthony even stopped practice to have me share my journey.

I share these times because it is important for anyone in the battle to have success and recognition. It is important to get and give honest sincere complements. We are all human and we never know when just that simple honest "I am proud of you" might make a huge impact on someone.

Side tracked again, back to the challenge. I made it 30 days averaging right at 33,000 steps a day which for me is right at 18.5 miles walked every day for 30 days. I felt great so I said to my wife and posted on Facebook that I was going to keep going on 30,000 steps a day for as long as I could. So 40 days passed, then 60 days, then day 71, July 10th, 2011. That would be the last day of my consecutive days of 30,000 steps. 71 consecutive days of at least 30,000 steps in a day. I was proud of the effort and relentless attitude I had during the 2.5 months. I averaged right at 18 miles a day, close to 32,000 steps. I walked approximately 2,343,112 steps for a rough total of 1,278 miles. That is the equivalent of walking from Seattle WA, to San Diego Ca, in 71 days.

I want to share with you what my days looked like. I had already begun working in Denver Co while living in Camas WA. I was typically in Denver for 8 to 14 days then home for 3. While I was in Denver the steps and mileage in some ways were easier to attain. I was there by myself so I worked and walked. I would get up at 5am each morning get breakfast and be out the door walking from 5:30 am to 8:30 am. I would typically get in 24,000 steps during that 3 hour walk. I would walk the same path each morning from my apartment to the foothills of the Rockies then about a 2.5 mile hike up the foothills then turn around and head home. By 9 am I was showered and in the car off to visit restaurants. I did all the little things to get in more steps when I could such as park as far from restaurant or store as I could. When I was eating lunch or dinner, if I was by myself, I would walk while I ate. When I was done for the night I would head home and download my steps into the BodyBugg program and if I was not at 30,000 I went for a walk or sometimes headed to the gym. Sometimes I was walking the neighborhood at 11:30 pm just to finish my steps. No excuses for me I was relentless to hit the goal of 30,000 everyday.

Travel days were some of the toughest days because I missed my family so much I did not want to have to walk for 4 hours when I would get home from my flight. So on travel days from Denver I would book the earliest flight home typically around 9 am. Then I would get to the airport around 4 am and walk the top concourse for 3 to 4 hours. The top concourse was for overflow passengers when flights were delayed so there was no restaurants or shops up there just a little over a quarter mile loop. I would put in my music and go to work. There were a few times I traveled I would get in my 30,000 steps at the airport, before boarding the flight. I was sweaty but it did not matter to me. Maybe to the person next to me on the flight though! Sorry at least I did not weight 360 pounds anymore. My goal each walk before my fight was 20,000 steps so I would still walk for a little while when I got home. I would typically walk with the family even on the days I already got 30,000 at the airport.

It was the same routine when traveling back to Denver except I did not walk as long at airport because I wanted to spend as much time with family as possible. I always tried to catch the last direct flight back to Denver. When I landed in Denver I went straight to the gym and would walk on the treadmill. By this time in my walking I could pretty much tell where I was in my steps each day just by the amount of time I had walked. I was always pretty close in my estimate before I would download my BodyBugg. Some may think I was bit overboard with my walking, but I was motivated, encouraged and having fun. It was tough being away from my wife and 3 boys so I distracted myself with walking and work. Besides great things came out of those 71 days and many seeds were planted. I can honestly say this book is being written because of what came from those 71 days. I love the saying "Ordinary people accomplish extraordinary things with extraordinary behavior's" I do not know who to attribute that quote to, but at the end of the day every single human on this earth is ordinary. It is our actions that make us extraordinary.

Chapter 16

"Are you willing to be a person of influence, or a person who is easily influenced?" Dale Rule

Day 72 was July 11, 2011 I woke up at 6 am to start my day of 30,000 steps. I realized for whatever reason, none in particular that I was done with that challenge in my life. Day 71 was the last day of consecutive days with at least 30,000 steps. My wife and 3 boys and our 4th non adopted son Chandler Box (Jeffery's best friend) were spending 6 weeks in Denver with me. The main purpose of the time in Denver with the family was to make the final decision on whether or not we were going to move to Denver. I do not remember what I told my wife that morning about me ending my walking streak just that I felt it was time to end it and give my body a little rest. We had also had a trip to Mount Rushmore and the Grand Canyon planned for the time we were in Denver and I knew during the days we were driving my streak would come to an end. So I rested that day or at least I did not go on an extended walk I should say. I was off of work that day, and we had made plans to go to the Denver Zoo.

While we were driving to the zoo I was listening to the radio and they were talking about a 24 hour radio-athon for a cause. I looked over at my wife who was driving and said to her "Lya do you think I could walk for 24 consecutive hours?" She glanced over at me and her exact words were "there is something wrong with you" she was chuckling when she said it, but I think in the back of her mind she really was wondering what was wrong with me. I kind of laughed at the thought as well and did not think about again for awhile, but God planted a seed in me that day. It is very interesting to me that I heard that on the radio and first thought about walking for 24 hours was on the same day I decided to stop my consecutive 30,000 step days. That seed that was planted on July 11, 2011 has resulted in my completion of three, 24 hour walks and counting. As I mentioned earlier we were very blessed to get to travel while we were in Denver with the family. I continued to walk everyday even when we were traveling but I would take an occasional day off here and there. My goals for walking daily did not change even when traveling. I typically walked six to eight miles a day, about a 2 hour walk. I planned my off days for when we would be in the car for the majority of the day.

The day we were leaving for the Grand Canyon I decided to take the 4 boys on a walk to tire them out. We had decided to leave in the early evening so Lya was going to take a nap while the boys and I walked. Then the boys would sleep for the majority of the drive. I had an awesome trail I wanted to take them on, lots of elevation changes. We had to climb a small mountain and hike down a canyon. It was beautiful in the foothills of the Rockies. I had walked that trail and numerous connecting trails plenty of times so I planned out a 13 mile round trip. I had walked that 13 mile loop three times averaging about three and a half hours each time. So I drive us to the trail head and off we go. Five and half hours later we finally get back to the car. I thought those poor boys were going to die. The boys had been hiking with me three to five days a week for about four weeks. We had been on some eight and nine mile hikes, climbed a lot of challenging trails, but nothing to that difficulty. This was by far the hardest one we had done and it took us a little longer than I had planned. About one and a half hours longer, but I was very proud of each of them, no complaining just pushing through.

Needless to say but we did leave a little later than planned. Lya was worried because of spotty cell phone coverage so she could not reach us, and we were gone longer than anticipated. I can say though, the boys and I slept very well.

I have one more foothills of the Rockies walking adventure to share. The area that I walked the most was about three and a half miles from my apartment west of the Flat Irons mall in Broomfield Colorado roughly 12 miles south of Boulder. I had not been working in Denver all that long so I did not know the area at all other than Map Questing where my restaurants were and some minor exploring. I had driven to the entrance of the trail and hiked part of it a few times. So one morning on a day off I walked to the trial from my apartment. I planned on putting in a solid 10 to 15 miles of walking/hiking that day. Little did I know 30 miles and close to 10 hours later I would make it back to my apartment! Leave it to me to get lost in the foothills of the Rockies and not really know anybody yet to call for help if needed. The trail is about a ten mile loop if you stay on the trail and do not cross the highway into the flat irons hiking area. The trail does cross two roads and circles around a lake and four cattle grazing pastures. You learn a lot when lost. I had hiked about two miles of trail on previous trips then turned around and went back to car. A lot of this trail is used by mountain bikers so I knew I was not going to die out there, but I did realize about three hours into walk I was lost. I had taken enough turns and different trails that I could not back track. Most important I never should have crossed the highway. My one saving grace was six white wind mills. I knew if I could continue to see them and eventually get to them, they were about six and a half miles from my apartment. I had driven by them and knew how to get home from there. I did not realize at first that the trails ran through cattle grazing areas. Twice I took what look like trails to the top of the hill which ended in dead ends at fences and unwalkable terrain, so I had to backtrack to the main trail. I walked to the lake area but it was private and fenced off. At one point I called my wife to tell her that I was lost and joked we might need to call the National Guard to find me. I had followed enough trails and walked far enough that I could see the city of boulder in the distance, that is how lost I was. It was a long adventurous day and I ran out of food and water. I had only packed enough for a short walk. Roughly 30 miles and 10 hours of walking/hiking on accident! What an adventure and to think that about 15 months before that it took me 41 minutes to walk 1 mile!

Chapter 17

"When you find yourself imprisoned other will listen!"
Pastor Dave McCabe

In August 2011 after spending 16 days in Oklahoma City and Tulsa developing three District managers, based on our families decisions not to move my Jack in the Box career came to an end. I flew home for good in August with my mind now fully consumed by the 24 hour walk. By the end of August the ball was rolling on the first annual 24 hour walk for Obesity and Multiple Sclerosis awareness. In truth for me the first walk was about surviving and making it the entire 24 hours. A great friend and former Jack in the Box colleague of mine Jeff Tennant jumped into planning and marketing of the walk with me. Jeff had already developed a website for me, everyonewalk.com, which is now the name of our non profit. I have very little skills around technology especially developing a website so I am very blessed to have a friend like Jeff! Just as important is Jeff's very patient wife Erika who puts up with me.

Jeff has had a lot of experience with the local media both with his own website and working for the local paper throughout college. Jeff and I put together a press release for the first walk and sent it out to see if we could generate some interest, the response was awesome. There were a couple of articles written about the event, I was interviewed on the radio before and after, and one of the local news stations sent out a camera man to interview me while I was walking. I actually had 2 news stations call me and apologize for not making it out to the event. I started my walk at 6am on a Sunday. It just happened to be that the Occupy Portland protest started the Friday night before so most of the local news resources were covering the protests. Other than the press release we did not really market the walk. I honestly was not sure if I could walk for 24 straight hours only stopping for restroom breaks and a few 10 minute breaks to eat and change shoes. I was concerned if we went overboard and I could not make the whole 24 hours I would disappoint people.

I did tell all the players and parents of the football team so word did get around the Camas area and there was an article written in the local Camas paper. Going into the walk I had very little expectations about how many people would walk with me at different times throughout the walk. I had not even thought about raising money through the walk until a parent asked me a couple weeks before the walk where they could make a donation. On the day of the walk I got to the track at Camas high school and spent the next 24 hours walking in circles! Yes I do the event at a track, like NASCAR except I change directions. I have been asked numerous times why at a track and the answer is, people need to know where to find me so we can walk together. Another reason is I always know where the bathroom is!

Here is a cool thing that happened before the walk. Talk about God putting people in the right place at the right time! As I was out looking for shoes and different things for the walk I went to a local store "Fit Right Northwest" now just known as "Fit Right." I had been to Fit Right a few other times in the past. After all I went through 10 pairs of shoes in the first year of walking and I now I go through a pair every one to two months. When I walked into Fit Right I was walking over to the shoe wall and this young man walks over to me and asks if he could help me. I had not even looked up at him yet, but I knew that the voice sounded familiar to me. When I looked up I realized I had coached this young man in football at Centennial nine or ten years ago when he was a freshman and a sophomore. So I said Ryan Vail and at first he just kind of stared at me like how do you know my name? I do not believe Ryan know who I was at first I was at least 100 pounds smaller than when I had coached him but he did recognize my voice and after a brief pause he said with a slightly questioning tone "Coach Rule?" I said yep it's me just half the size. It was so awesome to see Ryan. I love to reconnect with former players. One of the greatest parts of coaching is to watch these young men grow in life. Ryan himself is an amazing story. Ryan was not a real big kid as a freshman but boy was he athletic, physical, and smart. He might have been the smallest member of the freshman team but still was a starter for us on defense and rotated in all the time on offense. Ryan stopped playing football after his sophomore year in high school because he became an elite distance runner. I do not know if Ryan was a competitive runner before high school but by the end of his senior year he was one of the top runners in the country and earned a scholarship to run at Oklahoma State University. Now Ryan is a top distance runner for the U.S. team and one of the top marathoners in the world. Funny I remember him as a 5'5" maybe 100 pound cornerback and receiver not afraid of anyone. I share about Ryan because I am very proud of him and all he has achieved. I am blessed to know Ryan, and also because Ryan gave me some of the most important advice about my walk. Something that I would have never thought about that saved me a lot of pain. As Ryan and I were discussing the walk Ryan asked me where I was going to walk so I told him around a track. Ryan then told me that at least every 2 hours I needed to change directions as I went around the track. If I did not change directions I would destroy the hip that was facing the inside of the track. Small simple advice from an expert! Ryan worked very limited hours at Fit Right due to his training and running commitments. If I had not walked in there that day more than likely I would not have seen Ryan and there is a very strong possibility I would not have been able to finish the walk. Thank you Ryan for taking the time to share your expertise with me! I am very proud of all you have and will accomplish in life.

Back to the walk; I set a personal goal to walk 75 miles which is equal to 300 laps in lane 1 around the track. I carried a clicker counter with me and counted every single lap I walked. 75 miles is roughly 143,000 steps for me so I had my BodyBugg on as well to get double confirmation on my total miles walked. The walk went amazing and I had at least one person walking with me for 23 of the 24 hours I was walking. There are so many I want to thank, but I have to mention two by name. The first is Debbie

Eagle. Debbie is our head football coach Jon Eagles amazing wife. Debbie came to walk later at night somewhere around 11pm on Sunday. When Debbie came I had been walking for around 17 hours already. Debbie is a nurse and gave me outstanding advice on taking care of myself, hydrating properly, and eating, as well as making sure I was ok. Debbie walked with me for at least an hour. Thank you Debbie for caring enough to make sure I survived. It was about an hour between the time Debbie left and my cousin showed up. It is the only time in 3 walks I have walked by myself.

Chad Schiffman my cousin showed up sometime between 1 and 1:30am to finish the walk with me. Chad pushed, pulled, and encouraged me all the way to the finish. The hours Chad was there were the hardest. I was exhausted, hurting, and borderline delusional. It was dark and cold out plus my body is use to being in bed from 1am to 6am, not walking. I thought I was ready for what I would go through, I was wrong. Physically and mentally that was the hardest thing I had ever done. It was amazing, gratifying, and personally very motivating, but it was brutally hard. That 24 hour stretch of time changed the path that my life was on. We had over 100 people walk through out the first event and many people came out more than once throughout the 24 hours to walk. I did accomplish the most important goal of the 1st walk for me personally. I finished and lived to tell about it. I missed my mileage goal of 75 miles but I did make 71 miles a little over 133 thousand steps in 24 hours which was 284 laps around the track. Just as important I learned some valuable lessons about training for walks to come. I also learned what to expect physically and mentally from the grueling event. We raised a little over $1000 and gave it all away to M.S. and the football team.

I want to share the finish of the walk it was so amazing around 4:45 am I started to see head lights coming to the track and by 5:15 there was between 25 and 30 players, students and parents to walk the last 45 minutes with me. Not only did the sun coming up re energizing me but to have so many people care enough to get up early on a school day to finish the walk was amazing. Special thanks to the Krecklows, Dustin and Andrea who put in serious mileage in support of their aunt who passed away from M.S complications. Not only did they walk during the day but came back to walk the end of the event. At 6 am I crossed the finish line exhausted and excited. I got home at 6:30am after Lya and the people there picked everything up at the track. I jumped in the shower and got ready to do a radio interview before I could go to bed. After the interview Monday morning around 7:10 am I hit pillow and passed out.

2011 football season was an interesting year for me I was helping where ever I was needed but mostly I was working with one of the best high school defensive coordinators around, Dan Kielty, and the outside linebackers while being the "D" coordinator for the J.V. team. My primary responsibility was J.V. defense and we had a J.V. game that night, Monday at 6pm. Do to some unforeseen circumstances on our freshman staff that year I ended up helping with the defense during practice and calling "D" for freshmen games as well. It just so happened that we were able to schedule an extra freshmen game for Monday at 4pm against our neighbor school Washougal high. So I had a double header the same day my walk ended. I slept until 3pm dragged myself out of bed, grabbed some food, and headed to Washougal high about 20 minutes from our house. I was definitely sore and tired but overall my body was in great shape. The biggest issue was my feet. They did not blister only had one small blister. They were very swollen and hot to the touch. I had trouble putting my shoes on they were so swollen. This lasted about three days and it felt like I was walking on hot coals.

I got to the freshmen game about 10 minutes before kickoff at Washougal high and as soon as some kids saw me the whole team stopped warm ups and clapped as I walked over to the sidelines. All the players and coaches were coming over to me and high fiving me and telling me congratulations and how proud of me they were. It was a very humbling and awesome experience. I called the defense for the first half of the game, and the first 2 defensive series of the 2nd half, I had leave the game to get to the J.V. game at Camas High.

Periodically during both the J.V. and freshmen games while we were on offense, I would sit down on the bench.

Adrenaline and emotion go a long way but, I was exhausted. I left Washougal high about 25 minutes before kickoff at Camas which should have gotten me there about 10 minutes before the game started. Of the many times I have driven between the schools this was by far the longest time it had ever taken me to get to Camas high. As I pulled up to the entrance gate to Cardon Field at the high school there was no close parking places and we were lining up to kickoff so I knew we would be on defense first. I did not even park in a space. I parked next to the fence by the gate, locked the car, and literally ran to the field. Not the smartest thing to do but I had to be there to call the defense. As I get to the field the starting defense was running out on the field and looking back for a defensive call when they all realized I was running onto the field. They all stopped and came over to me, giving me high fives and hugs as were the players on the sideline. Joe Hallead our head J.V.

coach came up and gave me a great big hug and told me how proud he was. Joe had walked for numerous hours Sunday night at the walk. It was once again a very humbling and awesome moment. As they game got started, when the first play was being run I heard a commotion from the stands, I looked over and all the parents were giving me a standing ovation and clapping along with the players.

It was incredible and emotional memory I will never forget. To get to share it with all three of my boys, my oldest who was a sophomore on the team and my two youngest who were helping on the sideline, as well as my amazing wife who was in the crowd clapping with everyone else it was very inspiring. I learned a lot about myself and my faith in the 40 hour window from the start of the walk to the end of the J.V. game. I truly can do all things through Christ who strengthens me. I definitely learned "you must accomplish something mentally before you can physically".

Chapter 18

"Impact what you control influence what you do not!"

Dale Rule

The second annual 24 hour walk took place in September 2012. One of the things I learned from first walk was finishing at 6am was tough. I was the most exhausted when my body was used to sleeping. So I started the walk at 10am and moved it to begin on Saturday versus Sunday. We had a few changes to the second walk none bigger than making the walk a senior project for two of the seniors on the football team. Huge thanks to John Norcross and Troy Patterson for being the first seniors to take on the senior project. You both are incredible young men with amazing futures and you are both an inspiration to me. The way we set up their senior projects was for them to help with marketing of the walk then be the host for the event. I told them both that they did not need to be there for the entire 24 hours, especially at night when I was walking, but they both refused to leave. They slept in tents or in a lawn chair, sometimes in the men's bathroom where there was a heater as it got below 40 degrees that night. The two main focuses of the walk each year is Obesity and M.S. awareness. So the boys each took one of the causes and became subject matter experts and did their board presentation on obesity and M.S.

The second big change was the formation of everyonewalk.com a 501(c) 3 nonprofit committed to fighting the obesity epidemic in the U.S. It was never my vision on February 10, 2010, when I was 335 pounds and thought I was going to die walking 1 mile, to start a nonprofit that will influence and impact our great nation on the obesity epidemic. I was trying to save my life, God had other plans. I learned how to take something I had to do and turn it into something I loved to do. One of the biggest reasons initially for starting the nonprofit was because people wanted to donate money to the walk. I did not want to be personally responsible for other people's money. We give it all away any way and now we are legally protected and they can get a tax write off. I need to thank Dave Madore for introducing me to the most amazing lady, Patricia Johnson and her team at Ministry 911. I could not have afforded to get my nonprofit started without your help, blessing's and prayers.

The goal for this walk was 82 miles in 24 hours. An increase of 11 miles from last year's total about a half mile more per hour. I had learned a lot from the year before and trained different, and harder than the previous year. My wife and I are polar opposites on some things and how I set goals really shows it. Each year she has told me to set the goal to finish the walk and whatever the mileage is, it is. She worries that when I set such a tough goal that I will push myself to an unhealthy place to achieve it. I love her for it! She keeps me grounded but also understands why I set goals each year. I can honestly say I don't know if I could finish the walk each year if I did not have a goal. A tough goal to stretch me, the walk is very hard mentally and physically. Besides you have to accomplish it mentally before you can physically.

At 10am I set off to get 82 miles which is 328 laps around the track and approximately 160,000 steps. Well I missed the goal again but I pushed hard and finished at 79 miles, eight more miles than the previous year. I was very pleased with the improvement and I had 45 to 50 minutes were I did not walk. (Will explain) I finished at 316 laps around the track and a little over 150,000 steps. What an amazing day it was and the event grew over the previous year. Again we had some great media attention most notably a very flattering article in the Columbian sports section written by Paul Valencia. Paul not only wrote about the walk but wrote about my weight loss journey. I remember talking with Paul before the interview and I asked Paul to make the story about the seniors and Paul very matter of fact said to me "Dale I will include the boys in the article but the story is about you and what you have accomplished and continue to accomplish." Then Paul said to me "Dale your story will impact people" which it did. The response to the article was overwhelming and I was very blessed and empowered by the feedback. Not only were Paul and the paper getting great feedback, but we had people calling the Athletic Director at Camas high complementing me and the school. Thank you Paul for sharing my passion with others!

We more than doubled the amount of people who

walked at least once throughout the 24 hours from the 1st walk. More important to me is that I had never met at least half the people who walked. The previous year I knew 95% of the people who walked on a first name basis. I want to give a quick shout out to Coach Joe Hallead for the 2nd year in a row he walked his tail off. Both years Joe walked between 12 and 17 miles with me. Thanks for your belief in my actions Joe. So many amazing people and experiences and stories from people I could write a book just on the participants from the walks. I do want to thank my cousin Chad Schiffman again who was there in the middle of the night once again pushing me through the hard times.

I was very honored to spend a considerable amount of time walking with the Mayors of both Camas, Scott Higgins and Washougal, Sean Guard. Behind every great moment and movement stands a group of impactful and influential people. Scott and Sean you are part of that group for me and my vision. Scott your continued support, belief, and encouragement in me and my goals are uplifting and I am honored to represent the city of Camas in my journey. To walk with these 2 men and hear their passion and vision for our cities was inspiring. Both mayors walked at least 13 miles.

At one point in the early evening Lya and I were walking together and I looked out on the football field and there was at least 50 to 70 high school and 10 middle school kids hanging out. Some kids were just sitting down talking, some were playing catch, and some were setting up tents to spend the night. My two youngest sons Jeff and Josh had friends from school and their football teams and they were running around the field. One interesting group lead by my oldest son Joey decided for the second year in a row to see how high they could stack the tractor tires that we use for training. They had 10 big tractor tires and there were 10 to 15 football players working/playing together to stack them up. It gave me some entertainment to watch, but they did get them all stacked up. I said to Lya this is why I do this event. This is what the walk is all about bringing communities together. Not everyone is heavy or obese but everyone knows someone, a family member, a friend, or a colleague that struggles with weight and their overall health due to weight related causes. Every kid that came to the track that day walked and at some point introduced themselves to me and thanked me for what I was doing.

Every one of us can make a difference one step at a time I am no different than anyone else I am as ordinary as it gets. I just developed some extraordinary behaviors! Then I surrounded myself with people I never want to let down. I have had people call me a role model and each time I thank them for the compliment, but I disagree, I cannot live up to the standards we put on what we call a role model, the pedestal is so high so the fall is very far and we all fall. In my personal belief there has only been one role model and there will only ever be one role model and that is Jesus Christ. The only one ever worthy of the pedestal! I would rather be called an example. An example you can learn from both the success and the failures, and we are all human so we will all fail at some point. Every action has an impact on yourself and/or someone else, so what's your impact? An example is just an ordinary person with extraordinary behaviors. To me an example is someone willing to fail so they can grow, and trust me I have failed many times, and I am still willing to fail. A role model for me is to be immolated, looked up to, and revered there has been only one Jesus. Example's are to be learned from, but never glorified. Duplicate the good and learn from the not so good.

Got side tracked again, back to the walk. Many kids spent the night at the field in tents, sleeping bags, lawn chairs, or wherever they fell asleep. No coed tents, my wife was in charge! 98% of the walk went perfect, 2% was frightening. The weather was great and weird at the same time typical northwest day. I got a sun burn during the day and it was below 40 at night. I believe that big swing in body temperature played a role in my 2%.

A little background I realized after the first walk I needed to eat more food throughout the day even if I did not want to. I lost 16 pounds during first walk with drinking water consistently and eating what I thought was a good amount of food. So Lya and I had a plan for me to eat minimum every three hours even if I did not feel like eating, not including occasional snack of fruit and whatever the kids would bring me. The plan was going great for the first half of walk I felt great. Then around 8pm my cousin Kim brought me the most incredible bbq steak and I ate the entire plate while I was walking. Following our eating schedule I had a sandwich, some fruit, and a cookie at 7pm. I had put away a fair amount of food in about an hour but I was burning a lot of calories so I was fine.

The mistake I made happened around 8:45pm. Matt Lang, our youth pastor, and Dave McCabe our senior pastor at Grace Foursquare put together a free burger feed at a local restaurant for the football team. Matt had asked me earlier in the day if I wanted a burger from the event and I said yes that would be great. When Matt was done at the restaurant he headed back to the walk with a bacon cheeseburger and fries. When Matt got there around 8:45 pm he met me as I came around the grandstand area of the track and gave me the burger and fries. If I would have thought about it I would have waited a couple hours then ate the food but instead I ate it as I was walking. So between 7pm and 9pm I had a sandwich, some fruit, a cookie, monster plate of steak, and a bacon cheeseburger and fries. As I write this I realize as scary as it sounds I have eaten this much food in one hour's time on many occasions while sitting around watching TV. I guess that is one way to get to 363 pounds! Anyways, I was burning so many calories, at least 14,000 calories at each walk I was not worried about how much I was eating. The problem was after eating so much in such a short time I stopped eating all together. I also cut back my water intake, not sure why.

Between 9pm and 1am I did not eat or drink anything, not good! Around 1am a group of football players came to the track with a bag of food from Taco Bell. At 1am I took a 10 minute break, ate a bean burrito, and drank some water. After the short break I got back to walking. Around 4 am I was not feeling very good. So I went and sat down under the canopy where my wife was sleeping. As soon as I sat down I knew something was wrong. I immediately was light headed and felt like I was going to throw up. I got up and walked about 10 feet to a light pole to lean on it and throw up in the grass. My cousin Chad was there walking with me so he got Lya and they both came to see what was wrong. I was leaning on the pole dry heaving because I did not have anything in me. From 9pm to 4am, 7 hours, I had eaten 1 bean burrito and had about 16 oz of water. I had walked at least 24 miles in those 7 hours. That was not very smart on my part. Learned a valuable lesson that night!

As I was leaning on the light pole before Lya and Chad got to me I was already yelling for Lya. I knew something was seriously wrong. As I was leaning on pole I was starting to black out. It was one of the scariest moments of my life. I asked Lya to get me some food. I walked about 6 feet to a fence that is 5 feet tall and draped my arms over the fence so I would not fall down. I was so weak as I started to fall backwards the sweatshirt I was wearing caught on the fence around my armpits, the only way I did not collapse. I was terrified and even writing this now my heart is racing just thinking about it. My mind was racing everywhere. Were they going to have to call an ambulance? Can I finish the walk? Was I going to die? It was that scary. Lya brought me a bagel and Chad was there holding me up. Lya helped me take a bite of the bagel it was a little hard it had been out for a while, but as soon as I started to chew and food was getting in my system I was already feeling better. I was very dehydrated so it was very tough to swallow, but the little I could was already making me more alert, it was amazing how quick I responded. By this time

John Norcross and some of the other boys were up and helping me and Lya. I could not eat any more of the bagel it was too tough to swallow and Lya was already peeling me an orange. I was still at the fence but able to stand on my own while holding onto the fence. I drank some water and ate half the orange and was moving around. I went back to the canopy to sit down, finish the orange, and drink some more water.

After about five minutes at the canopy I was feeling much better. I got up to start the walk again but Lya had other plans! Lya gave me 2 choices, go home and end the walk or go into the bathroom were the heater was, relax and eat and drink more. Lya said I had to be in there for a minimum of 30 minutes then we would decide if the walk could go on. I agreed to go into the bathroom. I was not really thinking all that clearly and was still a little weak. The boys helped me into the bathroom and a group of us hung out by the heater. After sitting for about 20 minutes I wanted to get up and move around a little to see how I was feeling and so I would not cramp up. I got up and started to move around and for the next 20 minutes I walked in circles in the bathroom. After about 40 minutes Lya and I talked, I felt really good so we decided I would finish the walk. Thanks to Lya, Chad, John, Troy and many others that were in the bathroom for taking care of me.

I had about 5 hours remaining in the walk when I got back on the track and I was feeling really good. I promised Lya I would not push myself at crazy pace to try and hit my goal and that I would eat every hour and drink water every 30 minutes. When Lya puts her foot down I better listen, I love you so much! The last five hours went great. I finished strong felt great, and learned a valuable lesson. The walk ended at 10am on Sunday. I got home at 10:20am, jumped in the shower, and headed to church at

11am. Once church was out I got home around 12:30pm, went to bed, and passed out until 10:30pm. I had to work at 11pm at Safeway throwing freight.

I want to take a moment and share my work life with you during the time of my 2nd walk. This is just another part my story, my life, and my journey. No excuses just doing what I had to do to provide for my family. Trust me I if could have done things different work wise I would have.

I had already been working at 24 Hour Fitness for 10 months. I was working 30 hours a week there. In August I got a job at Fed Ex Express and Safeway in the same week. At Fed Ex I was working 22 to 25 hours a week unloading planes, and at Safeway I was working five graveyards 36 hours a week throwing freight. Add to all those hours the approx 25 hours a week for football and for 11 weeks I averaged working 116 hours of work a week. On the weekend of my 24 hour walk I got home and to bed from football at 11:30 pm on Friday and started the walk at 10am on Saturday and was back at work Sunday night at 11pm. From early August until Christmas day the only day off I had was the day of my walk. Christmas Day thankfully all my jobs were closed. I would drive from job to job or job to football and often sleep in my car for one to two hours at a time. I would pack a cooler in the back of my car and that is what I would eat from sometimes for two or three days at a time. I would shower sometimes at 24 Hour Fitness because it would be a day or two before I would go home. It was brutal but I had a family to support. I share this season of my life to say no matter the obstacles if the prize is big enough the price is never too big.

I learned some big lessons from this walk. Awesome relationships and connections were formed through this walk. One of those relationships was with our Mayor Scott

Higgins. Scott is a Camas kid raised in Camas and a graduate of Camas high. Scotts commitment to Camas and the residents of Camas is awesome I am blessed to call Scott a friend. One of the questions Scott asked me while we were walking was "why is this walk not held at Doc Harris?" Doc Harris is the athletic stadium down in town by the old high school. My answer to Scott was I do not know. I had asked after the first walk if it would be available to do the second walk at "Doc Harris" and the impression I got was that it would be a very hard sell to get it moved there. So I half jokingly said to Scott you are the Mayor you, could make it happen. Scott answered very clearly with "we will have the walk at Doc Harris next year" which we did!

Chapter 19

"Behind every great moment or movement there is a group of impactful and influential people!" Dale Rule

The 3rd annual 24 hour walk was at Doc Harris just as Scott said it would be and what an incredible adventure it was! There were a lot of expectations around the state for our football team at Camas High. We had played in the semi finals the year before losing to the eventual state champion and we were returning around 80% of our starters. We would enter the season as the #1 ranked team in the state of Washington. When Lya and I were planning the walk for this year I already knew our football schedule for the 2013 season. Our first game of the year was against Jesuit high school in Portland Oregon. Jesuit is a powerhouse program in Oregon with multiple state titles, when they came to our place in early September 2013 they were the #1 ranked team in the state of Oregon. Knowing the magnitude of this game I talked with Lya about starting the walk 30 minutes after the game ended. We were playing at Doc Harris that night and the walk was at Doc Harris so it worked out perfect. After Lya and I discussed it for a few days I wanted to talk to our head coach Jon Eagle and get his blessing on doing the walk after the game. I never want the walk to take away from these young men, they all work very hard. It is their time and the last thing I want to be is a distraction. As I was talking with Coach Eagle he told me he thought it as a great idea so Lya and I went to work on the details.

There were a few changes this year for the walk. Every year we try and learn from the previous year's walk and make the changes to continue to grow the event. This year I actually ended up with four seniors doing their senior project on the walk. Adam Dawson took M.S., Taylor Kauffman took obesity, Dallin Bradshaw was event coordinator and marketing, and Drew Clarkson with a special addition to the walk. I was very blessed and honored to have the opportunity to use the walk as a platform for one incredible young man with a very inspiring story.

Drew Clarkson was a two year starter on the offensive line entering his senior year. Drew was drawing attention for his talents from multiple colleges eventually committing and signing a full ride scholarship with Oregon State University. Drew's story is not mine to tell but I will give a few details to explain why I opened the walk up to Drew as a platform to bring awareness to Drew's story. In early 2013 Drew found a lump on one of his testicles. Drew was diagnosed with testicular cancer as a junior in high school and had surgery to remove his testicle. Drew then underwent chemo with one big goal to return just a few months later for his senior season of high school football. Not only did Drew beat cancer and survive chemo, he was back on the field at the start of the season and led us to the state title game. Drew is an incredible example and leader. In the early summer shortly after Drew's final round of chemo, I approached him in the weight room during summer work outs and asked him what he was doing for his senior project. Drew told me he did not know yet so I asked him if he would like to use the 24 hour walk as a platform to bring awareness to testicular cancer. After Drew talked this over with his parents he jumped on board thus becoming the fourth senior on the project. Now the 2013 24 Hour Walk was to bring awareness to Obesity, M.S., and Testicular Cancer.

Once again the walk went amazing and once again I learned some valuable lessons for walks to come. We had our first ever event sponsor. A big thank you to Darwin Rusu for coordinating a sponsorship with Wilbur Ellis. We had numerous local companies involved with donating, and pledging. Again I set a mileage goal a pretty aggressive goal to walk 100 miles equal to 400 laps. That is roughly 192,000 steps in 24 hours I would have to walk at an average of 4.16 miles per hour in order to reach 100 miles.

I want to thank the following people and companies for their involvement in the walk. First my amazing wife Lya, who will not go home and sleep even when I beg her to. Lya takes care of everyone who comes to the walk and constantly takes care of me. Another thank you to Shannon Lambert for helping Lya for so many hours. Fit Right and their owner Dave Sobolik. They had me professionally fitted for shoes then donated the shoes and compression socks as well as Dave giving a financial donation, thank you Dave and Fit Right Team. Dave has supported all three of the walks. Rachael Peterson with RP Imagery for your support and the amazing video you shot and posted on the everyonewalk.com site about my story. Video Only and Wade Forner provided us with two huge televisions for the day of the event, which we had college football playing on all day. We had four Portland Trailblazer dancers come out and walk for an hour and take pictures with anyone who wanted them.

A very special thanks to Don and Alison Lovell with "The Barbers" who made a significant financial pledge for each mile I walked, but also offered to double the pledge if the Camas Mayor Scott Higgins walked 30 miles throughout the 24 hours. Thank you Don and Alison you both have selfless, servant hearts towards youth and youth athletics, you both are incredible examples for us all to follow, thanks and God Bless. Mayor Higgins you are a mentor for me, you inspired me when I watched you push yourself to not only achieve the 30 miles but to exceed the 30 miles in one day. You gave me motivation to push through even while I was overcoming my own obstacles. I knew you were exhausted watching you walk down the straight stretch of the track and veering from lane one to lane five and back to lane one as you went around the turn, but there was no quit in you. I want to once again thank Paul Valencia and the Columbian. Paul your article detailing Drew's story was incredible and inspiring as well as promoting the 24 hour walk again thank you Paul. Dan Trujillo with the Camas Washougal post record first walking with me for an hour after the game, then the great write up on the walk thank you Dan. Thank you Jim owner of Jimbo's Deli in Washougal for making a $500 donation. And the numerous individuals and families who made pledges and donations, as well as coming out to walk. We more than tripled the amount of people who walked with us this year!

I was very fortunate to have the opportunity to interview in person on two different radio shows on 750 am "The Game" by 2 great men. It was a very interesting, slightly scary, and exciting experience for me. Chad Doing and "Flight 750" team thank you for having me and allowing me to share my story, passion, and vision. Chad thanks for asking the tough questions that people want to hear the answer to, and only one of them got me in trouble with my wife! John Canzano I want to thank you for the time on "The Bald Faced Truth" as well, but most important I want to say to you that I look up to you and your incredible wife Anna. The Bald Faced Truth Foundation is such a blessing to so many families and kids. I was honored to give a portion of the money raised at the walk to your foundation as I will every year going forward.

John and Anna you have such an incredible reach through your careers and both of you use it to give back to kids and families that are less fortunate. Your passion for others is admirable. I am blessed to know you both and looking forward to being involved with the BFT Foundation for many years to come.

Back to the walk, I am going to start with the training leading up to the walk. As I shared I set an aggressive goal of 100 miles. I typically walk eight to fifteen miles every day averaging one rest day every two weeks but I knew this would not be enough mileage a day to prepare me for my walk. About seven weeks before the walk I started to increase my speed and mileage. Here is the challenge to the training for the 24 hour walk this year. I had shoulder surgery to repair a torn rotator cuff nine weeks before the walk. I promised my doctor I would not walk for two straight weeks after surgery that left me seven weeks to train for the walk. By the way those two weeks were the first time in four years that I had taken more than two consecutive days off of walking. I had to wear my arm sling for five weeks after surgery so I trained for the walk with the sling on for three weeks then had it off for the last four weeks. Those four weeks are the only weeks I had to train with no restrictions from the doctor, but my movement was definitely restricted from the surgery. Even with the sling I was putting in heavy mileage, many days twice a day. Once the sling was off the biggest difference was the pace I could walk at. I knew I had to average 4.1 miles an hour for 24 hours to hit the 100 mile goal. I had to train at that speed. I had to put in heavy mileage at a faster pace often pushing my walking speed above 4.5 mph for hours at a time. My shoulder was sore and tight, and my walking gate was always changing. I was attacking my physical therapy to heal as best I could before the walk. It was just another obstacle to overcome or potential excuse if I gave into it, but there would be no giving in! I trained harder in the weeks leading up to walk than I have ever trained for anything.

During my daily walks year around I walk between 3.8 and 4.1 mph and typically walk two hours on work days and will walk longer on days off. During my training for this walk I was putting in an average of three hours in the morning and three hours in the evening. I was taken off all three of my jobs due to shoulder surgery so the only time commitment I had to work around was football practice. I found the inability to swing my arms at a fast pace even after sling was off put a lot of force on my legs. Especially when I was really pushing the speed I was walking at. My shoulder was definitely an obstacle I had to overcome in my preparation for this year's walk.

Throughout my training leading up to walk I worked

on numerous different plans on how to reach the 100 mile mark. Knowing full well the last four to five hours at the pace I needed to push would be much harder than the previous year's walks. I finally settled on the strategy to walk the first hour to hour and a half at my normal pace 3.8 to 4.1 mph until midnight. I wanted to get my body warmed up and be able to visit with the people who stayed after the game to walk with me. With the walk being 30 minutes after the game I knew there would be a lot of people still there to begin the walk with me and there was at least 50 at the beginning. I also knew starting so late at night I would have some time when there was not as many people walking so I could put my music in and pound out some miles. I walk faster with music I my ears. My plan was to have four to five miles in by midnight then put in music and over the next 10 hours get as close to 50 miles as I could. It was a very aggressive, but doable plan that would put me at roughly 54 miles with 13 hours remaining. If I could hit the goal I would only need to average 3.5 mph for last 13 hours to hit 100 miles. My heaviest mileage would be at night when I was by myself just me and my music it would also be when I was my freshest.

So the plan was in place training was going great, had a sponsor for the walk, we had raised money and had numerous people already pledging money for each mile I walked. The seniors were excited and promoting the walk, we had big screen TV's with live feeds, blazer's dancers were scheduled to participate. The city of Camas was on fire for the epic football game between the two top ranked teams in Washington and Oregon. I was very blessed to be interviewed in person on two different radio shows as well as have the Columbian run an amazing article on Drew and the walk. Shoulder was doing pretty good for just having surgery on it eight weeks earlier. Everything is perfect right? I am in the best physical shape since high school.

Then Saturday comes along, six days before the walk, when I get out of bed to get ready for football practice my left hamstring feels like it is turned sideways! It is so painful I cannot fully straighten out my leg. I can feel a knot half way up hamstring on the inner part of my leg. I go into immediate repair mode! I get out the foam roller and go to work on my leg. No walking this weekend. I had already planned to take Tuesday as a light day and Wednesday off. Then have a good walk on Thursday and relax as much as possible on Friday before getting ready for the game and the walk. Everything changed with the hamstring acting up. It was odd I had not done anything at anytime leading up to Saturday were I felt I had hurt myself. It felt like I had a bad cramp in the middle of the night and I could not get it to release. As I shared earlier cramping is a way of life for me. This was the some of the worst muscle pain I had ever felt, it hurt to do anything. Get out of bed, walk up stairs, you name it, it hurt to do it. I did as little as I could. I needed to get it better before Friday. Every chance I got I was foam rolling to try and get the knot worked out. I remember as plain as day on Tuesday evening we had the football kids out do a fundraiser blitz for the team. A few of us coaches were waiting back at the school to collect for the blitz. I was sitting on the side walk foam rolling and I felt the hamstring muscle release. It felt amazing, but even with that I was going to be very careful leading up to walk only three days away. I was, for the first time, a little nervous about the walk and the pace I needed to walk at. Wednesday went great, I even went for a walk at a very casual pace with no big elevation changes.

Thursday was going great until I was at the freshmen football game calling the defense. It was the first high school football game for both teams and all these kids had only been a team for about three weeks so it was a little rough at times. We had scored late in the first half to make it 7-0 at half. It was a great defensive battle from both teams. Then a lightning moment happens like it can so often in football. I get very involved emotionally into coaching. My wife thinks I am a little crazy, the kids laugh at me, but it's good and I love what I do. Late in the 3rd quarter we stop Jesuit and force them to punt. One of our player's Vinnie makes a great move after catching the punt, the other 10 guys do their jobs and down the sideline he goes for a touchdown to put us up 14-0. I react during the play and take off running down the sideline with the players. By the third step my hamstring is in a knot again almost taking me to the ground. Not very wise by me, but I get a little excited. So back to foam roller and ice I go. I have 30 hours to get it as healthy as possible.

Now its Friday day of the game and walk, I learned a big lesson that day. I thought I would be able to sleep during the day. Not a chance! I was up at 6am on Friday and did not go back to bed until 11:30pm on Saturday. I was 'up 41 hrs, spoke at the school assembly about the walk, did a radio interview, had all the emotions of the game and the walk, was injured, and tried to walk 100 miles in 24 hours. Biggest lesson for me never start the walk at night after a game again. The walk is brutal enough but to try and do with no sleep just added to it. The game was amazing one the biggest crowds ever at Doc Harris, media everywhere, college scouts, and I think almost the entire town of Camas what an incredible atmosphere for those young men. We won big with a running clock the entire second half because we were up at least 40 points. It was a great start to a historic season. Running clock was great news for me it meant I could get a few extra minutes of rest before the walk started which it turns out I needed to get my hamstring tended to by our trainer.

I had already spoken with our trainer Brady Corse before the game about wrapping me up before the walk. Neither Brady nor I knew the extent of the injury to my hamstring before he checked it out to wrap it. As Brady was examining my hamstring he told me my hamstring was so tight it felt like a solid bone with a knot in the middle of it. Brady then strongly suggested that I not walk that's how bad the injury was. There was no way I would not do the walk. I would literally have to be to the point where my legs could not move in order to not walk at the event. Too many people had put in too much time and effort for me not to walk. I knew I could walk. I had been on my feet most of the day already. I had Brady wrap it up I said a prayer and off I went.

I decided to try and stick to the game plan I already had. I just was not sure how fast I could walk. The wrap on the hamstring was a huge help, I probably would not have been able to walk 50 miles if I did not have it wrapped. I honestly knew deep down once I started to walk that it would be very difficult to hit 100 miles. It was tough to get a big fast stride with my injury. But I was definitely going to try as hard as I could. The plan stayed true to course at the beginning. The walk started at 10:30 pm so I walked with people that were there and still averaged close to 3.8 mph pace. Then at midnight I put in my music and off I went. It was at that point that I knew for a fact I could not maintain a 4.1 mph pace for 24 hours. I walked the next 4 hours as fast and as hard as I could by myself with music going. I must have been going pretty fast because I had two different people come up to me on Saturday and say that they tried to walk with me during the night and could not keep the pace. One big thing that I noticed with the leg wrapped was that my gate was different. This was causing soreness to muscles in a different way than normal.

At the 5.5 hour mark I decided to unwrap my hamstring and see how it felt. When I first took the wrap off I had to have my wife help me stand up it was so weak and wobbly. For about the first five minutes of walking it felt like it was going to give out when I would step without it wrapped. As I continued to walk without the wrap it started to feel a little better, but I was walking about half as fast as I walked with it wrapped. After an hour of walking with it unwrapped I had my amazingly patient wife rewrap it for me. Another important lesson came from this injury. I believe if I would have been physically able to walk the 54 miles in 11 hours as originally planned, I am not 100% confident I would have been able to walk 46 miles in the last 13 hours. My concern is the 10 hours at a close to five mph pace would have taken too much out of me to finish the 13 hours at a 3.5 mph pace. That is a lesson that I will take into the 2014 walk. With the injury to my hamstring, I got into the pattern of walking 2 hours as hard as I could with hamstring wrapped and then 1 hour at a recovery pace with it unwrapped. This pattern of two hours hard and one hour of recovery pace actually lead to me being physically fresher and mentally more alert during the last four to six hours versus the previous two years walks. The only downfall to rewrapping the hamstring after a one hour break from it being wrapped is that each time I rewrapped it my gate would be different because when wrapping it with a compression wrap it would have different pressure points each time.

This walk wreaked havoc on my body much more than the other two walks combined. My hip on the side of my injured hamstring took the brunt of the force and it took a good 4 weeks for my hip to heal. My feet blistered very badly because of the ever changing gate in my walk. Even with all I went through physically at this walk I look forward to attacking the 100 mile goal in 2014.

So how far did I walk in 2013? At the seven hour mark I was very happy where I was for total miles already walked. During the four hours from midnight until 4am I walked a little under 20 miles almost a five mph pace. So at seven hours I was a little over 30 miles walked. I set my half way mark at 45 miles this is where the two hours hard and one hour recovery really paid off. I had five hours to walk 15 miles. That is a three mph pace. At 12 hours I hit 45.2 miles 181 laps around the track. I was very confident I could duplicate that effort over the next 12 hours and hit 90 miles in 24 hours. Besides the sun was up, it was warm out, I felt sore but great. So the goal was set to 90 miles. I stuck to the plan two hours as hard as I could with leg wrapped 1 hour unwrapped to recover. With one and half hours to go I was on pace to hit 90 miles.

Then I decided to push it as hard as I could to see if I could go a little higher than 90 miles. I am not sure what fast looks like after walking for 22.5 hours and being awake for 38 hours but I had a group of around 30 adults and 20 to 30 kids walking with me during that time and they were laughing at me and my silliness, I was definitely a little delusional. At the 24 hour mark I had not only hit my 90 mile mark but exceeded it by one mile finishing at 91.25 miles for the 24 hours. Twelve miles further then the year before. 365 laps around the track approx 175,000 steps, roughly the distance from Vancouver Washington to Mt Hood in Oregon. I was happy, blessed, sore, and exhausted.

Chapter 20

Believing in others until they can believe in themselves!

I share these moments in my journey not to brag or look pat's on the back. I share them in hopes that I can encourage more people just to get out and move. You do not have to walk 90 miles in a day or even 1 mile but just do something. I can honestly tell you if I thought for one minute the 24 hour walk had no impact I would not do it. The first one would have been the last one. It is not easy! At times it is not fun and I ask myself at each walk at some point, why I am doing this? The walk for me mirrors life. Full of different emotions, pain, and occasional self doubt, and ending with the feeling of accomplishment just like the journey of losing weight and keeping it off. No short cuts, be willing to earn it. It's a willingness to push one more step, one more mile even if in pain. Pushing through for others even when you think you are at the end of your rope. It's about taking your eyes off yourself and putting them on others. Believing in others until they can believe in themselves! The PRIZE being so big that the PRICE is worth the work. Do not set out on your journey to lose weight but to gain life! Your will to live must be greater than your want to give into temptation! One of my favorite sayings is "Impact what you control, influence what you do not." That is my goal with the 24 hour walk and everyonewalk.com. Truly the only thing I control is the decisions I make and the reaction I have to the decisions others make.

My goal is to influence through my story and my 24 hour walk. It is never my goal to motivate people. Motivation wears off as soon as we get distracted by life.

Through my influence I hope to impact some of the decisions people make. I have said too many people if I can walk 91 miles in a day you can walk 1 mile for 91 days. Here is what I believe, there will days were you walk more. Maybe 1 mile more, maybe 2, maybe 10 but at least 1 everyday that to me is making an impact through influence. You will have to move your attitude from I have to, to I want to, and I get to. You have to create the Prize for yourself then you can determine what the Price to attain it looks like. To me living is a pretty good Prize. Seeing my kids grow into men, have families, play with my grandchildren, be able to care for myself and not be a burden on my children or on society. This world needs your story! The successes and the setbacks! There are people you can reach that I never can. It's your time to step up for more than just yourself, but you must start with yourself! You're PRIZE, your path, your journey, no one can write your story.

Chapter 21

"Sometimes in order to have miracles in your life you have to do the ridiculous" Chad Veach

I recently had the privilege to hear Chad Veach speak at our Church. Chad made a comment that stuck with me. Chad said "Sometimes in order to have miracles in your life you have to do the ridiculous." That comment is exactly why I will continue to do the 24 hour walk every year until I physically cannot, because I do believe in miracles. I do have faith and belief, but faith and belief without action is a wish or a delusion. We are in trouble with obesity and weight related illness in this country and these facts are very evident in the info I will share shortly, but these facts do not even begin to cover the cost that extra weight and obesity have on someone's feelings of self worth and perceived value to others. I will do the ridiculous all while praying it impacts the miracles. The miracles are you. You standing in the gap where others are not ready or willing to stand. You making a difference for yourself so you can influence others.

Everyonewalk.com is our nonprofit. I would like to share with you my vision of where I would like to take the nonprofit. I know there will be changes to the Prize as the Price/impact changes for the nonprofit. The goal is to have influence in all 50 states. My vision is to build Everyonewalk parks in every state then start to build multiple parks in each state. What is an Everyonewalk park? The more I dream about the park the bigger it becomes. I would like to get significant acreage and have it completely fenced in. Then have a safe all weather, covered (as needed) walking trail around the inside of the fenced perimeter. My vision for the park includes indoor and outdoor athletic fields, indoor and outdoor pools, community center, state of the art training facility, ropes courses, paintball field, batting cages, Frisbee golf, basically if you can play and get physical activity from it I want to provide it in a safe all inclusive environment. Here is the kicker, I want it to be free for everyone fully funded and supported through the nonprofit. Remember I am looking for miracles and I am willing to do the ridiculous!

Obesity is not a rich person or a poor person problem it is an everyone problem! Seven out of ten Americans are struggling with their weight! As of today obesity is the #1 cause of deaths and disability in America! If you are not personally fighting a weight battle you probably know people who are. If not all you have to do is look around everywhere you go. We are all in the battle when it comes to the costs we pay for medical insurance, due to costs in the billions spent every year on weight related illness and diseases.

Here are some statistics, trends, and projections on where we are and where we are heading if do not make significant changes. According to the National Center for Health Statistics, part of the Centers for Disease Control and Prevention "2012- 34.9% of adults were obese. Children ages 6-11 18% obese, Children ages 12-19 21% obese. In 2012, more than one third of children and adolescents were overweight or obese." Harvard research says that over the past three decades childhood obesity rates have tripled in the U.S. One out of six children is obese, and one out of three children is overweight or obese.

The US National Library of Medicine National Institutes of Health states the current trend forecast suggest that by 2030 51% of adult U.S. population will be obese and increase of 16% from 2012.

Harvard estimated annual health care costs of obesity-related illness are a staggering $190.2 billion or nearly 21% of annual medical spending in the United Stated. Childhood obesity alone is responsible for 14 billion in direct medical costs. In addition to growing health care costs attributed to obesity, the nation will incur higher costs for disability and unemployment benefits. Businesses are suffering due to obesity-related job absenteeism ($4.3 billion annually). Researchers have estimated that by 2030, if obesity trends continue unchecked, obesity-related medical costs alone could rise by $48 to $66 billion a year in the U.S. Obesity is closely linked with a number of health conditions, including heart disease, stroke, diabetes, high blood pressure, unhealthy cholesterol, asthma, sleep apnea, gallstones, kidney stones, infertility, and as many as 11 types of cancer, including leukemia, breast and colon cancer. No less real are the social and emotional effects of obesity, including discrimination, lower wages, lower quality of life and likely susceptibility to depression.

The bottom line: prevention is key to trimming obesity's high costs says Harvard University. "It is possible that a clearer understanding of the cost of obesity will spur larger and more urgent programs to prevent and treat it. While the U.S. has made some investments in the prevention, with the First Lady's "Let's Move" initiative", and professional sports promoting kids to be active 60 minutes a day. These efforts represent relatively small steps forward. Future public health prevention, funding, and communication remain under threat. To make an impact on obesity it will take the combined efforts of multiple individuals and companies. We do not have time for red tape, bottom lines, and stock prices! We are talking about a race that has to be won and won now, that is the human race. We the human race of this great nation are eating ourselves to death! We need a single minded focus from state and local governments, schools, nonprofit organizations, food companies, advertisers, professional sports leagues, and individuals. To make a healthier lifestyle the norm rather than the exception! These facts and trends are why we at everyonewalk.com are asking for your help!

These alarming facts and trends bring me back once again to why Lya and I started the nonprofit everyonewalk.com, just as John Maxwell said "One person can make a difference a team of people can make history!" That is my driving passion for the nonprofit and Everyonewalk park. As I shared I want to fully fund the park through the nonprofit. The number one way I would like to raise money for the parks is through monthly gifts from you, me, and everyone we know. Here is the hard sales pitch I am asking for a gift of $1 dollar a month equal to 12 dollars a year, just as important I am asking for your voice to help me share my passion and vision to build that team that will make history. I believe in the power of people! It is not going to take millions of dollars to impact this crisis it is going to take millions of people. I would rather have 1 million people give the gift of $1 a month then have a few people give millions of dollars. My goal is to influence millions of people who can impact millions more people rather than motivate a few people.

Chapter 22

The Prize IS worth the Price!

I would like to share with you some things that has had, and continues to have a great impact on my journey and my life. I am no professional these are just little tidbits I have accumulated through my life and for the first time I am really sitting down and putting some structure to them to share. Use what you can or like discard what you do not. Again this is just my story.

When I really began to take "Is the PRIZE worth the PRICE" personal for me was with my weight. I had to make changes. I was dying on the inside at 37 years old. As I shared earlier in the book I honestly believe that today 4.5 years into my journey if I had not started I would be over 400 pounds. I had to be ruthlessly honest with myself.

I had to share my desires, goals, and pain with somebody luckily I was blessed to have an incredibly patient wife. I had to trust someone I could be vulnerable and accountable to and they would be ruthlessly honest and accountable to me, again for me that was my amazing wife. I have learned through life as well as this journey that there are many steps to make lasting changes. The Price of change can be fluid but success is achieved when the Prize stays the same.

Let me ask you one question! Would you be willing to create the habits to lose one pound a week for one year? Think about it. Do you plan on living another year? I hope so! If you lost one pound a week for one year, you would be down 52 pounds! Take a moment, take the book with you. Go to the mirror and look at yourself and ask. How different would my life, my health, my attitude, and myself worth be exactly one year from right now? If I would commitment to lose just one pound a week for one year!

I want to share 3 points that encompass many steps for lasting change to occur

1. You must admit the addiction, vices, and struggles. -Why are you where you are? How did you get there, and how do you get out.

Energy flows were your attention goes and if you cannot admit the struggles your energy is spent on deceiving yourself. When you practice bad habits long enough they become the norm. Turn your energy to recognizing and getting out of the struggles so you can change your behavior's which changes your habits.

2. Recognize your traps, triggers, and excuses. -What are they for you? Emotion's, holidays, events, work, TV, family functions, traveling, I will start tomorrow/next week, it's too hard, I tried and failed, need help, no time, I am sick, do not know how to start, no money, vacation, I love food, I am lazy. Pick one, they all work. I know

because that is my personal list. I used every one of them at one time or another. You have to be aware of when you are most tempted and struggle the most. You need to talk to the person that is on this journey with you that will be brutally honest with you but yet will lift you up. You need a game plan for when those moments arise in your life both the planned triggers like holidays and vacations, as well as the unplanned like an emotional response. You cannot simply remove those desires when tempted you must replace them. I replaced them with walking. You must have a purpose and satisfaction "The PRIZE". You're WILL to live has to be greater than your WANT to give into temptation.

3. Replace the traps, triggers, and excuses with the truth.

-Arm and equip yourself. Who is you help? Where is your help? Are you transparent with your help? Define the Prize and Price to the smallest detail no surprises. You are the PRIZE! You are worth it! Your history is not your destiny. Your commitment and devotion today determines your destiny. Whose lives are impacted if you are not here? You are not a victim, a statistic, a label, or a title. Others need your story to save their lives! Many of them you have not even meet yet. What picture of you do you see down deep in the mirror past what you physically see? The Truth! You are a child of God and God does not make junk!

Your Prize must be defined and about you and you first. You have to be selfish about your health; your health is the ultimate Prize. Now what is the price you have to pay? Not the one you are willing to pay. Being ruthlessly honest with yourself what Price do you have to pay? What does it look like? By when? Will you get back up? Who is your support? Who will be brutally honest with you? Remember do not surround yourself with people who beat you up but people who build you up. Who will encourage you but not enable you? Who will aid you on this journey? If you do not have anyone, call me I will! You can do this I know because I did. You are the Prize and no Price is too big for you!

FINAL chapter: 23

"One person can make a difference; a team of people can make History!" John Maxwell

As I sit here at 4:38am working graveyard at 24 hour fitness. I share with you once again "The Prize is worth the Price!" In my life I have read maybe 10 books cover to cover. The majority of them were "John Maxwell" Leadership and Development books. Not a great thing to admit but in truth I have never been a big reader, that is changing as I grow. If someone would have told me that I would write a book I would have bet my life that it would never happen! I sit here 4.5 years after that first painful and embarrassing day of going for a 1 mile walk in 41 minutes a changed man by the grace of God and a lot of work. I have kept all the weight off and other than one 2 month stretch, have never put more than 15 pounds back on. Which by the way, in the last 55 days I lost 33 pounds walking, working out, and tracking my food daily. I am back to the weight I was at the last 24 hour walk. I am no one special, just surrounded by special people who impact, encourage and uplift me. Sometimes by their words, sometimes by their actions, many times they do not know I am watching. I am alive and healthy and the future gets brighter every day all because I went for a walk.

To my amazing wife Lya, next to Jesus and my salvation, you are the greatest gift and blessing I have ever received and ever will. Thank you for allowing me to be vulnerable, trusting me, allowing me to fail, and being an encouragement every step of the way. You are the rock of our entire family. You are an example for many women to follow, I love you. My amazing boys Joey, Jeffery, and Josh, I love you all so very much each of you brings joy to your Mom and me. It is so much fun to watch you grow into men. Men with great expectations on your lives but nothing you cannot handle. Thank you boys for allowing Dad to learn how to be a Dad! Allowing me to fail and then accepting my apology. Thank you for being young men of character and humility. Jeff Tennant the impact you have had on my life and will continue to have as we grow and grow the nonprofit, you are so selfless I could never repay you other than to offer my friendship and loyalty. Thank you for who you are.

To the thousand plus young men I have already been blessed enough to coach and the thousands more I will. The impact you have had on my life is immeasurable. To all the coaches I have been part of a staff with thank you for your commitment to developing the young men in this world and for so many of you pouring into my life. So many employees and peers thank you for trusting my craziness and passion. Many of you are my dear friends and hold a special place in my heart. Chris and Erin Loucks, Eric Johnson, and Tolva Miller we drove many miles together chasing dreams. Thank you for the memories I will cherish forever. Ed Thomas the stories we could tell, I love you my brother. Darrell my blood brother we went through a lot growing up but in the end always had each other's back I love you.

Arnie and Malia Jacobsen you poured into Lya's and my life as few ever have and we love you both very much. Jeff Kaneshige, David and Jennifer Locke, Matt and Sandi Tsuruda great friends and mentors at different seasons of my life thank you. Pastor Warren and Pat Willie thank you for all those days going out of your way to pick me up for church and sewing into my life! Mom, Dad, and Joan thank you for everything I love you all.

Jon Wolf you changed the course my confused, unsure life was heading in. Jon you opened your heart up to me.

First coming is as our head coach my senior year, then patiently developing me as an 18 year kid who wanted to become a football coach. Jon thank you for seeing something in me! Then trusting me enough to bring on at Madison, then recommending me to Chris Knudsen at Centennial.

Jon Eagle you are an incredible example and leader, thank you for allowing me to fulfill one of my dreams to coach my sons through high school. Thank you for trusting me I could never repay you for this honor it truly is a blessing to work with you. I guarantee I am missing people who have had an influence or impact in my life but please know you are thanked and loved. It is amazing when you take your eyes off yourself to see all the people placed in your life to make a difference. As John Maxwell said "One person can make a difference; A team of people can make History!"

Jesus, thank you for loving us so much that you made the ultimate sacrifice. You died for each and every one of us so that we could have eternal life.

I recently got asked "why do you walk?" This is a question I have been asked numerous times and have had different answers. All valid answers, all true answers, but this time I answered it different and truly from my heart and at the root of why I walk. I Walk to Live! Plain and simple I today and now for years have walked for many reasons, for myself and for others, but the bottom line simple truth is I Walk to Live. Live longer and live healthier physically, mentally, and spiritually. I don't make a major decision in my life without walking on it first. I pray when I walk, I rest in God's grace when I walk, I cry, laugh, and sing when I walk. I talk about life with my boys when I walk. I plan our lives with my wife when I walk. Sometimes I write a book when I walk. I dream about the impact on this world God has planned in my life when I walk. I dream about Everyonewalk Park when I walk. I walk 24 consecutive hours once a year to bring awareness obesity. Through all of this I walk to live, because as stated earlier I believe today I would be over 400 lbs today if I did not go for a walk. There is more to being alive than just breathing. Walking gave me my life back! I can play with my kids and one day my grand kids. I can play with my wife. I can coach football and be active coaching not just observant coaching. I can walk for miles, hours and even a whole day. I am blessed enough to inspire others to walk and live! So the answer to the question of why do you walk has many reasons but only one answer "I Walk to Live!"

15312540R00132

Made in the USA
San Bernardino, CA
22 September 2014